Understanding
Personality Disorders

Understanding Personality Disorders

An Introduction

DUANE L. DOBBERT

 PRAEGER

Westport, Connecticut
London

Library of Congress Cataloging-in-Publication Data

Dobbert, Duane L.
Understanding personality disorders : an introduction / Duane L. Dobbert.
p. cm.
Includes bibliographical references and index.
ISBN 0–275–98960–7 (alk. paper)
1. Personality disorders. I. Title.
RC554.D63 2007
616.85'82—dc22 2006028564

British Library Cataloguing in Publication Data is available.

Library of Congress Catalog Card Number: 2006028564
ISBN-13: 978–0–275–98960–6
ISBN-10: 0–275–98960–7

First published in 2007

Praeger Publishers, 88 Post Road West, Westport, CT 06881
An imprint of Greenwood Publishing Group, Inc.
www.praeger.com

Printed in the United States of America

The paper used in this book complies with the
Permanent Paper Standard issued by the National
Information Standards Organization (Z39.48–1984).
10 9 8 7 6 5 4 3

This book would not have been possible without the dedication of my dearest friend and colleague, Joyce Elaine Dobbert. Her careful reminders about skew kept my personal experiences at an arm's length. She is also the guardian of those afflicted with personality disorders. It is easy to identify the negative characteristics of the disorders, but much more difficult to understand that the afflicted persons developed their disorders at the hands of others.

These unfortunate persons were victims before they victimized others.

Contents

Preface

SCENARIO I

The first class of the first year of law school was beginning in 10 minutes and the atmosphere was charged with anxiety. Successfully completing an undergraduate degree, scoring solid on the LSAT, and acceptance into a tier-one law school was insufficient in elevating the levels of confidence of the new law students as they filed into the class. Regardless of the cum laude B.A. from a distinguished liberal arts college and a top 5 percent score on the LSAT, Lisa was nervous. She felt her heart racing, the shallow breathing, and the sweaty palms. It was so unlike her to lack confidence; but new ballgame, new rules. Lisa sat in the middle of the cathedral styled classroom and was pleased to observe that the other students appeared to be as anxious as she was. They were demonstrating the same uneasy mannerisms that she was. Attempts at conversation between the students were strained and cordial.

Shortly before the professor arrived, a handsome male student sat down next to her and began to disassemble his briefcase and assemble his laptop. Lisa greeted him cordially and he responded with a bright smile and cordial comment. The ice was broken and some of the anxiety began to subside. The student introduced himself as John and followed with the comment, "I am so nervous regarding this law school Socratic Method. I think I'll die if the professor calls on me first. They certainly didn't use the Socratic Method in my undergraduate school. Where did you do your undergraduate work?"

Lisa sighed with relief, the rest of the anxiety expelling in the sigh. "I'm so glad to know that I'm not the only one terrified of this first class period." The professor entered the classroom and the silence was instant. Brief introductions, explicit expectations, and the class was dismissed. John and Lisa engaged in relaxed conversation as they packed up and walked from the building. John inquired as to Lisa's schedule of classes and as expected, all were common, relatively typical of law school. Success is contingent upon study groups. Knowing no other students at that time, Lisa readily agreed to join forces with John.

John arrived earlier than Lisa to the next scheduled class and sat in the middle of the room. Lisa, nearly as nervous as she was at the first class, saw John and sat next to him. John smiled and said, "Shall we begin the study group tonight?" Lisa did not expect the study group to begin this quickly. Having not read the assigned cases, she suggested tomorrow night instead and John quickly agreed and asked, "Where and what time?" Lisa suggested they meet at 7:00 PM in the atrium of the law library and find a suitable location from that point.

John arrived at 6:45 PM and paced the atrium awaiting Lisa's arrival. Lisa arrived at 7:05 PM and quickly observed John's anxiety. "Is everything alright John?" "I was afraid you weren't going to show," replied John. Puzzled, Lisa responded, "Why would you think that?" "Because you were late, but I'm relieved to see you now."

During the course of the evening they planned a study schedule that accommodated Lisa's work and personal study schedule. Lisa was struggling to pay living expenses and trying hard to keep the educational loans in check. John was not working and living at home with his parents. They exchanged phone numbers, as well as residential and email addresses.

During the next class period Lisa suggested that they find a couple of more students to join their study group. John politely protested, indicating that he was fearful that adding additional persons would contaminate the learning milieu. Lisa, conversely, believed that four brains were better than two, but agreed to keep the study group small for now. The professor called upon neither Lisa nor John and both left the class relieved to have dodged the bullet one more time. They laughed and John walked Lisa to her car. "Would you like to go out for a cup of coffee?" inquired John. "Sorry, I have to go to work, perhaps another time," replied Lisa as she opened her car door. John could not hide his disappointment and replied, "Can't you skip work?" "Sure, if I want to get fired," was Lisa's retort.

When Lisa finished her shift as a waitress, she went home to read the assigned cases for tomorrow. By force of habit, she opened her email to find a message from John. "I apologize for trying to get you to cut work to get a cup of coffee with me. I hope you're not mad." Lisa had to think back to the conversation to recall if she had acted angrily toward him. "No, I'm sorry if I communicated that to you," replied Lisa.

The phone rang in 10 minutes and it was John inquiring if she had completed her reading and was interested in a having a beer and a burger at the local law student tavern. Lisa hadn't, but the idea of escape for a short period of time sounded wonderful. Lisa replied, "No I haven't, but I would love to get out for about an hour. The tavern is right around the corner." John indicated, "I know. I'll be waiting for you."

Lisa quickly changed out of her waitress uniform and walked around the corner. Ten minutes could not have elapsed, but John was already waiting in a booth. "I thought you lived across town. How did you get here so fast?" "I read your email on my palm pilot and I called from here," replied John. The scheduled hour was now approaching two AM and Lisa needed some valuable study time and sleep. John teased her about being anal and obsessive-compulsive about studying. Lisa rebuked him and left.

The phone was ringing as Lisa entered her apartment. She answered and John apologized for teasing her and asked if she was angry with him. Lisa said "No, but I do need to get some study and sleep. Talk to you later." Lisa had difficulty in sleeping as she contemplated John's comments and relationship with her. She was certain that she had not led him on and that the relationship was merely one of law student colleagues. At least that was her impression.

While the study group of two was working effectively, Lisa was concerned that John always agreed with her position and was constantly asking her for her advice on cases. Initially this made her feel confident, but as he continued to agree with her opinion, she began to worry about her accuracy. Perhaps John was not disagreeing with her to avoid an intellectual confrontation. Lisa needed more input; controversial opposing input. She recommended again that they find two more students to join their group. John's face blanked in awe and disappointment. "Why?" asked John. Lisa explained that they were too similar in their opinions and consequently could not understand opposing views. The requisite adversarial nature of law and jurisprudence was absent in their study group. Lisa indicated that if he did not agree to find other students to join their group, she would personally find another study group to join. Lisa was shocked by John's response.

"But you can't. I cannot do law school by myself. I need you."

John suffers from Dependent Personality Disorder and Lisa is the latest in a long line of victims who will fall prey to his disorder.

SCENARIO 2

The long 4 iron shot to the green drifted to the left and landed in the water hazard. Mark spun about and hollered at his caddy, "I told you not to make any noise when I'm swinging. Give me another ball. I'm hitting that shot over." The caddie quietly removed a ball from his pocket and tossed it to Mark. Mark's second shot landed softly on the green.

After the putts were dropped and the flag returned to the cup, Mike turned to the other members of the foursome and asked for their scores. Mark promptly indicated, "Par, Four." Mike rebuked him, "You didn't count the water-hazard stroke and the penalty. That's two in, three out, four on the green, and two putts for a six."

"Like hell it is! That damn caddie disturbed my swing. I'm not counting that water shot and I don't care what you say," Mark aggressively told Mike. "Then the bets off," replied Mike. Mark rushed across the green and informed Mike that the game was over as far as he was concerned and Mike was no longer welcome in Mark's foursome or crowd.

The locker room and grill were packed with sweaty, boisterous golfers. Mark was holding court, admonishing the behavior of his caddie, and boasting about the soft 4 iron that landed on the green. Mark was demanding that the caddie be fired. He also informed the club members that he was going to approach the "golf committee" to recommend some changes in the rules that provide "relief" for situations just like this one. "After all, who pays for this country club anyway? It's our club, not the PGA's. If the pro doesn't like it, we'll fire him too. Who's in this with me?" Not one member affirmed his agreement, but no one voiced opposition either. They were all too scared of public ridicule directed at them by Mark.

These country club members are just a few of the victims of the Narcissistic Personality Disordered Mark. All of Mark's family, friends, and associates are victims of his disorder.

This book is dedicated to everyone who is afflicted with a Personality Disorder, most of who do not realize it. It is dedicated to the relatives, friends, and acquaintances of those afflicted with Personality Disorders. It is also dedicated to those who are victims of a person afflicted

with a Personality Disorder. The afflicted persons, relatives, friends, acquaintances, and victims number in the millions. The *Diagnostic and
Statistical Manual of Mental Disorders*, Fourth Edition, Text Revision
(DSM-IV-TR) identifies ten specific Personality Disorders (APA, p.685).
The disorders differ greatly in diagnostic criteria and behavioral manifestations; however, they have two dominant themes in common. The
persons afflicted with these disorders are not mentally ill, and these
afflicted persons create unwilling victims.

Unless one specifically studies these disorders, they are unaware of
their existence and consequently, cannot identify these characteristics in
others. The relatives and acquaintances do not understand them, and the
victims do not see them coming. The general public observes persons who
demonstrate "strange" behaviors and remove themselves from perceived
threatening situations by avoiding these persons. The general public
crosses the urban street to avoid contact with the "homeless" person
begging for change, and the self-proclaimed prophet who is announcing
the "end of the world is coming." Their out-of-mainstream behavior is
frightening to some and annoying to others. Regardless, their behavior
is obvious and the general public avoids them.

The general public also avoids persons who are demonstrating aggressive, injurious behaviors to others. Public perceptions of dangerous
persons and locations are relative. The definition of dangerous is relevant to the individual's frame of reference. If one grows up in the inner
city urban environment, their tolerance for aggressive neighborhoods
and citizens is considerably higher than the person who is raised in a
single race/ethnic rural community. Conversely, city dwellers are cau-
tious of the backwoods' bars and their clientele. Regardless, the general
public avoids those persons and locations that they perceive as strange,
different, and potentially dangerous.

Persons afflicted with Personality Disorders are commonly found in
the mainstream. They do not look strange and their public behavior
falls within acceptable and tolerable parameters. However, they can be
dangerous. Persons afflicted with Personality Disorders always create victims. Victims experience physical, mental, and emotional losses. Victims
experience a reduction in self worth, unnecessary guilt, and emotional
trauma.

It is through the creation of these victims that the intrinsic needs of
the personality disordered person are met. Their actions have purpose
and intent. The pain and suffering experienced by the victim is premeditated. It is only through the creation of these feelings that the needs
of the disordered person are fulfilled. These disordered persons find no

fault with their behavior, and accept no responsibility for the victim's predicament or feelings.

In a sense they are self-centered and do not experience remorse for the pain and suffering they cause to others. Their world is egotistical; they are only concerned about themselves.

Further, they will not change their behaviors unless the consequence for their behavior is so personally painful that it exceeds the pleasure derived from the behavior. Consequently, they are solely responsible to themselves and do not care about their victims.

Virtually everyone has been related to, an acquaintance of, or a victim of a personality disordered person and nearly everyone does not realize it. They never see it coming and they don't know what happened after it's over.

This book will open Pandora's Box. This book examines each of the Personality Disorders and defines them in non-clinical terms. The characteristics and the behaviors of the Personality Disorders will be demonstrated and "become alive" through numerous scenarios similar to the two found in this preface. The scenarios will demonstrate the disorders in the perspectives of spouse/significant other, children, parents, best friends, employees, and employers. It is the intent of this book to "arm" the potential victims with knowledge about the Personality Disorders and the mechanisms of identifying them, understanding them, and, if necessary assist in finding a therapeutic intervention, or extracting oneself safely, with emotions intact. Further, the reader will be alert and will learn to avoid and/or control the actions of the personality disordered person.

In conclusion, this author offers a "truth in advertising" disclosure. You will identify people around you who are afflicted with varying degrees of severity of the Personality Disorders. They may be your spouse, your child, or your employer; but they will be there. If nothing else, this book will help you realize that you are the victim, not the person with the problem.

CHAPTER 1

Introduction to the Personality Disorders

The *Diagnostic and Statistical Manual of Mental Disorders*, Fourth Edition, Text Revision (DSM-IV-TR) (2000) discusses a group of disorders categorized as Personality Disorders. The DSM-IV-TR specifically includes ten different disorders in this category (p. 685). They differ significantly in characteristics and seriousness; however, they all possess certain diagnostic criteria in common. "A Personality Disorder is an enduring pattern of inner experience and behavior that deviates markedly from the expectations of the individual's culture, is pervasive and inflexible, has an onset in adolescent or early adulthood, is stable over time, and leads to distress or impairment" (p. 685).

Specifically, the American Psychiatric Association (2000) delineates the following:

General Diagnostic Criteria for a Personality Disorder

A. An enduring pattern of inner experience and behavior that deviates markedly from the expectations of the individual's culture. This pattern is manifested in two (or more) of the following areas:

(1) cognition (i.e., ways of perceiving and interpreting self, other people, and events)
(2) affectivity (i.e., the range, intensity, lability, and appropriateness of emotional response)
(3) interpersonal functioning
(4) impulse control

B. The enduring pattern is inflexible and pervasive across a broad range of personal and social situations.

C. The enduring pattern leads to clinically significant distress or impairment in social, occupational, or other important areas of functioning.

D. The pattern is stable and of long duration, and its onset can be tracked back at least to adolescence or early adulthood.

E. The enduring pattern is not better accounted for as a manifestation or consequence of another mental disorder.

F. The enduring pattern is not due to the direct physiological effects of a substance (e.g., a drug of abuse, a medication) or a general medical condition (e.g., head trauma) (DSM-IV-TR, p. 689).

A. AN ENDURING PATTERN OF INNER EXPERIENCE AND BEHAVIOR THAT DEVIATES MARKEDLY FROM THE EXPECTATIONS OF THE INDIVIDUAL'S CULTURE

This pattern is manifested in two (or more) of the following areas:

Cognition

Persons afflicted with a personality disorder commonly perceive themselves, other people, and events around them differently than viewed by others. They typically view themselves differently than others. They also view the people around them and events in light of that perception of themselves. Consequently, they have perceptions that are not necessarily accurate or accepted by others. Further, they demonstrate behaviors that are not appropriate or acceptable to others. These persons are considered to be ego-syntonic.

Webster (2001) defines ego-syntonic as "of or pertaining to aspects of one's behavior or attitude viewed as acceptable and consistent with one's fundamental beliefs" (p. 623). This is not an easy concept to grasp and understand. Persons not afflicted with a personality disorder generally have accurate and realistic perceptions of themselves and the world around them.

Non-disordered persons have fluctuations in their perceptions of themselves. These fluctuations are influenced by their relationship with events and other people. An individual with a normally realistic and strong sense of self-worth can be derailed by rejection and failure, but their self-worth will reinstate itself when future events and others provide positive support. Non-disordered persons also recognize and acknowledge emotions and behaviors that are not consistent or appropriate for particular events and generally control themselves accordingly.

Disordered persons, in contrast, view themselves differently than others do. They may perceive themselves in grandiose terms or may have a very low sense of self-worth, neither of which are accurate perceptions. These inaccurate perceptions of themselves influence their perception of events and consequently their behavioral responses.

These misperceptions develop in adolescence and solidify in early adulthood. They are chronic, that is, lifelong. Therefore, one must consider that the personality is stable, but ensconced in the personality disorder. Thus, the person will continue to view events and others in light of this skewed perception. These personality disordered persons view everything from their point of view, skewed as it may be. They are not capable of viewing the world from the perspective of another, nor are they capable of examining events from any perspective other than their own. Consequently, it is an egocentric view, albeit inaccurate.

The disordered person may view events that others view as benign differently. Further, they choose their behavioral response to the event from their inaccurate frame of reference. Others viewing the same event may consider the disordered person's behavioral response as inappropriate. Non-disordered persons are caught in awe of the behavior. They cannot believe that this person behaved in such an inappropriate fashion. Attempts to correct the behavior will result in confusion and a lack of understanding by the disordered person.

This is a difficult aspect to understand. The disordered person believes that their perception of the event and subsequent behavioral response are accurate and cannot understand how or why others find their perception inaccurate and their behavior inappropriate. The disordered person views and then acts according to their inaccurate perception of themselves. They are incapable of acting otherwise. Acting otherwise is incongruent, or inconsistent, with their personality. In order for them to adjust their behavior, they must change their perception of themselves. But they cannot change their perception of themselves because the personality disorder is stable and lifelong. Thus, even in the face of opposition and consequences, they will continue to behave inappropriately because they view the event inaccurately.

Affectivity

Persons afflicted with personality disorders also have difficulty in regulating the level of their emotional responses to events. They will either under- or overrespond. Their range and intensity of emotional responses are also apt to change. Coupling this inappropriate affectivity with the primary criterion of misperception of events and others results in behavioral responses that non-disordered persons find perplexing and often annoying.

An over-exuberant, aggressive response to a benign event is cause for alarm on the part of observers. Likewise, emotional hysteria is perplexing to others who view the event accurately. The misperception of self, events, other persons, and the subsequent inappropriate affectivity is dictated by the specific personality disorder and is the clue to diagnostic differentiation. Each personality disorder is described in detail in subsequent chapters and scenarios are utilized to clearly demonstrate the misperceptions in cognition and affectivity.

Interpersonal Functioning

The nature of the personality disorders influence interpersonal functioning. Non-disordered persons view events and other people accurately and, consequently, differently than the disordered person. This difference in perception produces a lack of understanding and often distresses the non-disordered person. Incapable of viewing the event or other persons from the skewed perception of the disordered person, the non-disordered person is perplexed and confused. The non-disordered person commonly examines their own perception of the event or other people for inaccuracy. Finding none, they begin to question the perception of the disordered person. Inquiry will result in conflict and interpersonal functioning is disrupted.

This disruption in interpersonal functioning may or may not result in distress for the disordered person. Distress is contingent upon the specific personality disorder. In circumstances in which the disordered person experiences distress, the subsequent behavioral response will be influenced by their difficulty in regulating their affectivity. Contingent upon the disorder, responses to interpersonal dysfunction may result in hostile, aggressive attack on one end of the continuum to self-destructive behavior on the opposite end.

Impulse Control

The misperception of self, events, and others, coupled with the inability to regulate emotional responses and the frequently encountered interpersonal dysfunction is exacerbated by a lack of impulse control. Rather than stepping back from the situation and examining the circumstances, the personality disordered person will respond impulsively.

The subsequent reaction by others to this impulsive unregulated response precipitates further interpersonal dysfunction and the circle continues.

B. THE ENDURING PATTERN IS INFLEXIBLE AND PERVASIVE ACROSS A BROAD RANGE OF PERSONAL AND SOCIAL SITUATIONS

Personality disorders have a sense of rigidity and afflicted persons are prone to be inflexible. They are not particularly responsive to change and are more apt to defend their perception of events and other people, rather than consider the possibility that their perception is inaccurate. Their particular disorder, the severity of the characteristics, and the perceived consequences of the event will determine the rigidity of their perception. In the absence of vigorous opposition or a number of persons questioning the accuracy of their perception, they will stand strong and vehemently defend their position. In the presence of mounting opposition and probable consequences, the disordered person will change tactics, which might even include a complete change of subject in order to escape with their perception intact. Following escape, the disordered person will examine the subsequent event and create an inaccurate perception that supports their opinion and dismisses the opposition's opinion.

This escape and creation of an inaccurate representation of the event reinforces the misperception of self and the circle continues. The disordered person does not change the perception of the original event, because they are unable to do so. It would be inconsistent with the personality disorder, and inflexibility requires adherence. If the person would truly modify their perception of the event, then they would not be afflicted with the disorder. The incapacity to correct the misperception is characteristic of the disorder, and the escape preserves the disorder. Modifications in behavioral response are utilized as a mechanism of manipulation, that is, escape and preservation.

This diagnostic criterion is also descriptive of the pervasive nature of the disorder. The personality disorders are not limited to particular aspects of an individual's life, but rather are found in all aspects. This is clearly understood when one recognizes that the disorder is the definition of the individual's personality. The afflicted person cannot have an accurate perception of oneself in one situation and then an inaccurate perception in another situation. The misperception of self is total and influences all aspects of the person's existence.

C. THE ENDURING PATTERN LEADS TO CLINICALLY SIGNIFICANT DISTRESS OR IMPAIRMENT IN SOCIAL, OCCUPATIONAL, AND OTHER IMPORTANT AREAS OF FUNCTIONING

As discussed in previous sections, the personality disorders precipitate distress in interpersonal functioning. This requisite diagnostic criterion demonstrates that the personality disorders precipitate distress and dysfunction in the important functional areas of an individual's life. As indicated previously, the personality disorders are pervasive and the cognitive and affective criteria are observable in different areas of an individual's life and daily routine. The behavior may be modified to fit the situation, but the behavior will always be driven by the misperception of self.

Scenarios are utilized with each personality disorder to demonstrate the presence of the disorder in different arenas of the afflicted person's life. These scenarios are discussed in subsequent chapters.

D. THE PATTERN IS STABLE AND OF LONG DURATION, AND ITS ONSET CAN BE TRACED BACK AT LEAST TO ADOLESCENCE OR EARLY ADULTHOOD

This fourth general diagnostic criterion for a personality disorder specifies that the disorder must be a chronic condition, one that has stabilized in the personality and was first manifested in adolescence or early adulthood. This criterion consequently excludes behavioral manifestations, which though similar to a specific personality disorder are not chronic, but rather temporary. Such behavioral manifestations may be precipitated by a variety of circumstances.

Trauma related to the death of a loved one, change in residence, employment status, and family structure, divorce, empty nester syndrome, etc., will precipitate changes in mood, cognition, interpersonal functioning, and impulse control. However, these changes are temporary and acute, and will dissipate with time, changes in the circumstances, and therapeutic intervention, if required. In contrast, persons afflicted with a personality disorder will exhibit the disorder's relevant criteria in an enduring pattern. It doesn't dissipate. The pattern of inner experiences and behavior will be pervasive and in a breadth of range.

This criterion also specifies that the disturbances in inner experience and behavior must have been demonstrated at least by adolescence or early adulthood. If the disturbance is manifested at a point later in life, it is more likely the result of another etiology.

E. THE ENDURING PATTERN IS NOT BETTER ACCOUNTED FOR AS A MANIFESTATION OR CONSEQUENCE OF ANOTHER MENTAL DISORDER

The behavioral manifestations identified as symptomatic of the personality disorders are not unique to the personality disorders. Rather, many of the inner experiences and behavioral manifestations are also symptomatic of other mental disorders. Consequently, the diagnosis of a personality disorder requires the careful examination of other mental disorders with similar symptoms. If the disturbances in cognition, affectivity, interpersonal functioning, and impulse control are better accounted for by another mental disorder, then a diagnosis of a personality disorder is inaccurate.

F. THE ENDURING PATTERN IS NOT DUE TO THE DIRECT PHYSIOLOGICAL EFFECTS OF A SUBSTANCE (FOR EXAMPLE, A DRUG OF ABUSE, A MEDICATION) OR A GENERAL MEDICAL CONDITION (FOR EXAMPLE, HEAD TRAUMA)

The sixth and final general diagnostic criterion for a personality disorder specifies that the inner experience disturbance and behavioral manifestations must not be the product of substance abuse, prescribed medication, or injury or disease associated with the brain. Changes in cognition, affectivity, interpersonal functioning, and impulse control may be precipitated by the use and abuse of illicit drugs and alcohol. Medication prescribed for a medical condition may also precipitate symptoms that imitate a personality disorder.

A persistent personality disturbance may be the by-product of a general medical condition. This is differentiated from a personality disorder by a marked change in the normative behavior of the individual. This marked deviation demonstrates that the disturbance in inner experience and behavior is not stable in the personality, but is a product of the general medical condition. General medical conditions that may produce a pattern of disturbance include brain tumors and Alzheimer's disease.

Subsequent chapters are dedicated to each personality disorder and the discussion of disturbance in inner experience and behavioral manifestations is explored clinically and exemplified through the use of scenarios. Each personality disorder is examined in relationship to disturbances in cognition, affectivity, interpersonal functioning, and impulse control.

CHAPTER 2

Paranoid Personality Disorder

PARANOID PERSONALITY DISORDER SCENARIO

At 4:30 PM, Donna observes her close friend and colleague, Millie, talking with their supervisor. Not Millie too, pondered Donna. She had just confided in Millie that the supervisor reprimanded her for an emotional outburst at another employee, accusing them of going through her work on her desk while she was out for lunch a week ago. Donna knows that a group of coworkers have formed a conspiracy to discredit her work and have her fired. Donna had previously discussed the matter with the supervisor who dismissed it as "hog wash." His attitude infuriated her and since then she refused to acknowledge his existence. It was obvious that she would have to deal with the problem herself and when she found her work disturbed, she challenged the coworker in the adjacent cubicle. Her loud emotional outburst was heard by all, and even as the coworker pleaded innocence and ignorance to what she was referring to, she heaped accusation upon accusation until the supervisor called her into his office and reprimanded her. Another outburst like that would result in her termination.

Donna knew that she was the talk of the break room and everyone was staring at her and giggling as they talked amongst themselves. This had been going on for a week and the anxiety was influencing her work performance. She thought about discussing it with her husband, but he was so distracted lately. He acted like she wasn't even there. He was sullen at dinner and spent every evening in his workshop or down at the corner tavern with his friends. Knowing that her concern regarding the conspiracy would fall upon her husband's deaf ears, Donna decided to tell her last remaining friend and coworker, Millie. She asked Millie to join her for lunch and told her the entire conspiratorial story. Millie tried to calm Donna, but Donna would have nothing to do with it. Donna was certain that this group was trying to get her fired.

As quitting time finally arrived, Donna approached Millie and demanded to know what she and the supervisor were talking about. Before Millie could respond, Donna began calling her a traitor and told her she would never speak to her again. Millie's alleged violation of confidentiality assured Donna that Millie was part of the conspiracy and she would treat her like all others; she would alienate herself from Donna and feel sorry. Donna could hold a grudge longer than anyone she knew. She would wait for Millie to come crawling back begging for forgiveness. Donna created a scene by storming out and slamming the door behind her.

Upon arrival home, Donna began to prepare her husband's favorite dinner. He would arrive just about 6 PM. Donna was anxious to tell him about Millie's actions in telling the supervisor about the conspiracy. At 7 PM, Donna's husband arrived home, only to find a demanding Donna. She wanted to know where he was and why he hadn't called to inform her that he would be late. Before he could open his mouth to tell her that he had to finish the automobile he was working on because the customer needed to use it in the morning, Donna accused him of "whoring" around. Not willing to stand and take another verbal battering, he spun on his heels and walked out, informing her that she needed help and if she didn't get some, he was leaving her. Donna rose in fury and threw an ashtray at him as he walked out the door. Donna determined that he was involved in the conspiracy as well and was probably having an affair with Millie.

Donna is afflicted with paranoid personality disorder.

The American Psychiatric Association identifies "the essential feature of the paranoid personality disorder is a pattern of pervasive distrust and suspiciousness of others such that their motives are interpreted as malevolent" (DSM-IV-TR, 2000, p. 690).

The APA delineates the diagnostic criteria as follows:

A pervasive distrust and suspiciousness of others such that their motives are interpreted as malevolent, beginning by early adulthood and present in a variety of contexts, as indicated by four (or more) of the following:

1. suspects, without sufficient basis, that others are exploiting, harming, or deceiving him or her
2. is preoccupied with unjustified doubts about the loyalty or trustworthiness of friends and associates

3. is reluctant to confide in others because of unwarranted fear that the information will be maliciously against him or her

4. reads hidden demeaning or threatening meanings into benign remarks or events

5. persistently bears grudges, i.e., is unforgiving of insults, injuries, or slights

6. perceives attacks on his or her character or reputation that are not apparent to others and is quick to react angrily or to counterattack

7. has recurrent suspicions, without justification, regarding fidelity of spouse or sexual partner. (p. 694)

Caveat

It is significant to inform the audience that the paranoid personality disorder differs from schizophrenia, paranoid type. The American Psychiatric Association identifies

the essential feature of the paranoid type of Schizophrenia is the presence of *prominent delusions or auditory hallucinations* (emphasis added) in the context of a relative preservation of cognitive functioning and affect. Delusions are typically persecutory or grandiose, or both, but delusions with other themes (e.g., jealousy, persecutory, or somatization) may occur. The delusions may be multiple, but are usually organized around a coherent theme. Hallucinations are also typically related to the content of the delusional theme. Associated features include anxiety, anger, aloofness, and argumentativeness. (pp. 313–314)

The paranoid personality disorder may be precursor to the paranoid type of schizophrenia; however, it is significant that in the absence of prominent or auditory hallucinations, a diagnosis of schizophrenia, paranoid type, is inaccurate.

Suspects, without Sufficient Basis, That Others are Exploiting, Harming, or Deceiving Him or Her

In the absence of evidence, persons afflicted with paranoid personality disorder assume others are interested in doing them harm through attack of deception. They believe that others are in a conspiracy to bring them harm and this delusion is extended to the belief that these persons have already harmed them through their conspiratorial nature. This delusion prohibits the afflicted persons from developing close relationships with others. They are difficult to live with and, consequently, friends and relatives often avoid them.

Is Preoccupied with Unjustified Doubts about the Loyalty or Trustworthiness of Friends and Associates

Friends and relatives who do attempt to maintain close personal relationships with the person afflicted with paranoid personality disorder are constantly required to demonstrate their loyalty and trustworthiness. The afflicted person is so suspicious of others that they are confident that even those who persist to demonstrate their loyalty are suspects. The associate who has a conversation or lunch with another demonstrates their lack of loyalty to the afflicted person. Grown-up children who fail to call every day or invite their in-laws over for Sunday dinner have demonstrated their lack of loyalty and the afflicted person feels grievously harmed and the delusion is reinforced.

Is Reluctant to Confide in Others because of Unwarranted Fear that the Information will be used Maliciously against Him or Her

The delusional belief that others are disloyal and untrustworthy precludes their ability to confide in others. The afflicted person believes that the information that they provide in confidence will be later utilized to bring them harm. The mother who fails to inform her adult children of her cancer is reluctant to do so because she believes that the children will utilize this information for their own exploitation and gain.

This inability to confide in others is a self-defeating behavior, as they lose the potential for important assistance and also distance themselves from others who are truly concerned and interested in helping. The elderly parent who will not divulge economic status fails to utilize the valuable assistance of adult children willing to assist in tax preparation, etc. The afflicted person believes that divulging that information will be used against them in the future.

Reads Hidden Demeaning or Threatening Meanings into Benign Remarks or Events

This particular criterion is a probable precursor for a diagnosis of paranoid type of schizophrenia. Casual comments or inquiries about the person's health are misinterpreted as conniving. Failure to invite the elder parent to a grandchild's soccer match in the pouring rain is misinterpreted as a lack of loyalty. Regardless of the logical explanation and demonstrated concern for their well-being, the afflicted person is affronted. Casual compliments are viewed as a manipulative ploy to gain favoritism. As these misinterpretations increase in severity, one must consider the possibility of a diagnosis of schizophrenia, paranoid type.

The subsequent action of the concerned family members to refer the person for a mental health evaluation reinforces the perception of maliciousness and they often feel irreversible injury. It is a tragic dichotomy for the family members. Attempts to provide love and concern are misinterpreted as acts of conspiracy and exploitation, and referring them for a mental health evaluation demonstrates the inaccurate truth to the afflicted person.

Persistently Bears Grudges, that is, is unforgiving of Insults, Injuries, or Slights

The person afflicted with paranoid personality disorder also has a tendency to maintain grudges against those persons that they believe have been disloyal or have insulted or slighted them. The mother who is not invited to Sunday dinner when the in-laws are invited will hold a grudge against the adult child and spouse. She fails to recognize that there have been numerous times when she has enjoyed Sunday dinner at the adult child's house without the in-laws present.

A forgotten or even late birthday card will initiate a grudge and the hostility may last for an extended period of time. They are constantly on the alert for signs of the expected hurtful behavior, and even the most benign insignificant and unintentional mistakes produce gross overexaggeration and again, the reinforcement that she cannot trust this friend or family member. They are slow to forgive and the real victim of the harm is the family member or friend who must deal with the alienation.

Perceives Attacks on His or Her Character or Reputation that are not Apparent to Others and is Quick to React Angrily or to Counterattack

The constant state of expectation that others are preparing to hurt them, the afflicted person, in anticipation of the hurtful behavior has defense mechanisms in queue. In situations where no others find a person's behavior insulting or injurious, the afflicted person misinterprets the remark or behavior and reacts with hostility, and commonly counterattacks. The angry counterattack is swift and emotionally painful to the unsuspecting friend or family member. The afflicted person reacts with hostility, and leaves, and initiates the long-term grudge and alienation.

Has Recurrent Suspicions, without Justification, Regarding Fidelity of Spouse or Sexual Partner

This criterion precipitates the inability of the afflicted person to maintain a long-term intimate relationship. The expectation of untrustworthiness is directed at the spouse or sexual partner. Vigilant in anticipation of infidelity, the partner of the afflicted person is subject to interrogation for being late home from work, an exclusive event planned with social or work acquaintances, or out of town travel. The afflicted person displays extreme jealousy and strikes out at same sex acquaintances that are flirting, from their delusional perspective, with their spouse or sexual partner.

These behaviors are the source of dissolving partnerships and marriages. The situation is exacerbated when the spouse or sexual partner denies the allegations of infidelity and attempts to involve the afflicted person in a therapeutic intervention.

Etiology and Course

It is significant to note that certain behaviors that are symptomatic of the paranoid personality disorder do not automatically justify the diagnosis. Persons who have experienced racial, cultural, ethnic, and/or gender discrimination are not distrustful of others because of the disorder, but rather their experiences. Consequently, they are neither suffering from paranoid personality disorder nor schizophrenia, paranoid type. Women working in a male-dominated profession are not paranoid; they are reacting to the reality of discriminatory practices and sexual harassment. Their distrustful attitude is directed at the source(s) rather than randomly discriminating. It may also be manifested in the form of anger and hostility.

In contrast, persons with paranoid personality disorder are distrustful in many contexts, particularly in competitive environments. They are apt to blame others for their failure to succeed and claim discrimination and conspiracy. Their chronic state of distrust for others forces them to be strongly independent. This independence coupled with the chronic distrust of others is frequently manifested in a state of seething anger and hostility. Frowns rather than smiles dominate their faces and a sense of unhappiness dominates the atmosphere around them.

One must also contemplate the origin of paranoid personality disorder in the modeling of the behavior. Internationally recognized developmental psychologist, Albert Bandura (1977), suggests that children can learn behavior by observing it rather than directly experiencing it. A child growing up in an environment with a paranoid personality disordered parent may learn the behavioral symptoms of the disorder by observing it in the afflicted parent. The American Psychiatric Association indicates that

paranoid personality disorder may be first apparent in childhood and adolescence with solitariness, poor peer relationships, social anxiety, underachievement in school, hypersensitivity, peculiar thoughts and language, and idiosyncratic fantasies. These children may appear to be "odd" or "eccentric" and attract teasing. In clinical samples, this disorder appears more commonly diagnosed in males. (DSM-IV-TR, 2000, p. 692)

Unfortunately, persons diagnosed with paranoid personality disorder, are poor candidates for therapeutic intervention. This logically flows from their chronic state of distrusting others.

CHAPTER 3

Schizoid Personality Disorder

SCHIZOID PERSONALITY DISORDER SCENARIO

Andy just preferred to stay in his room. His music, computer games, and the Internet were all he needed for pleasure and excitement. He couldn't seem to understand why his parents and siblings continued to bother him and call him a hermit. He wasn't hurting anyone, including himself. Andy was completely content.

The "loner" behavior began during his middle school years. Andy was considered "shy" during elementary school, but when coerced by his teachers, would participate in classroom and playground activities. He even started participating in cub scouts because his mother agreed to serve as "Den Mother" for his den. He wasn't as silly as the other cub scouts and didn't demonstrate the hyperactivity that the other boys did. Andy enjoyed working on the wood and ceramic projects. Andy could spend hours painting a ceramic figurine. When left to his leisure decisions, Andy would always opt to build a plastic model of an automobile or an airplane in his room. He could spend endless hours playing with his models. His parents considered his behavior as artistic and described him as more mature than his peers.

Andy became more solitary as he entered middle school. No longer was he in the same classroom with the same teacher every day, but rather rotated through six class periods with different teachers and commonly different students. He was not required to participate in class activities at the same level as in elementary school. As long as he completed his homework and was not disruptive, the teachers would just let him be himself. Andy listened enough to understand the homework assignment and appeared attentive; however, he was in a dream world miles away from the classroom. Andy didn't dream of hitting the winning home run, or traveling to exotic locations; he just dreamed of being alone and enjoying his solitude.

Andy, by choice, chose to be alone. Subsequently, he had no friends or acquaintances. He ate his lunch at a table by himself. He would commonly do his homework during the lunch break, and thus would not have to take any homework home. While he longed to be alone in his room, he did not exhibit anxious behavior. He would calmly wait for the final bell, drop his books off at his locker, and sit in any abandoned seat on the bus. The other middle school youths would celebrate their joy at the end of the day, chattering with their friends and running about in frenzied activity. Andy would sit quietly amidst the chaos of the school bus, calmly exit at his stop, and walk directly home. While his siblings would chatter with their mother upon arrival, Andy would cordially greet her with a hug and then go to his room under the guise of a great amount of homework to accomplish.

As the eldest, Andy was presented with a computer video playstation on his twelfth birthday. Andy graduated from model planes and cars to the world of playstation games. Andy never spent his allowance and gift money on trivial items; rather he saved the money for new games. He was also a regular customer of the local public library, checking out every available game. Interestingly, Andy was not interested in those games of contest with another player, rather he preferred those he could play alone. Andy spent every available minute in his room, playing video games and listening to music. His parents gave up attempting to involve Andy in outside group activities: scouting, athletics, church group, etc. His brother and sister were active enough to keep the parents running from athletic events, to dance class, to band practice. Andy was not a problem. He had respectable grades, good citizenship reports, and finished his chores at home. He was considerably less troublesome than his active brother and sister. Andy's parents decided to ignore the problem. They left well enough alone. They determined that Andy would embark on a career characterized by scholarly endeavor.

School was a different story. Andy was constantly the subject of his classmates' ridicule. The ridicule was brutally incessant, but it did not appear to impact Andy. He just ignored the ridicule and even acts of aggression. Andy would walk about without any expression. Eventually even the most persistent bullies left Andy alone. They found victims that responded to their abuse with at least some emotion. Andy did not express emotions of happiness or joy either. It was very obvious that the only activity Andy enjoyed was being alone in his room, but even when forced to leave his room and participate in family activities, he remained expressionless.

While in high school, Andy's grandmother died. She was deeply loved by all and the wake was a scene of intense grief: tears, cries of sorrow, and testimonies to her loss by all. Andy was without expression. He did not weep, talk, or frown. He was the same as always, unaffected by the circumstances imposed upon his life. Excused as his private mechanism for grieving, Andy's parents permitted him to seek refuge in his room throughout the remainder of the wake and internment. Andy barely smiled when he locked his door to intrusions and turned on his video game.

As time proceeded, Andy's grades went from exceptional to marginal, and his parents' expectation of scholarship went by the wayside. Andy would not attend the university, but would eventually settle on with a low-paying job in a manufacturing company. Andy jumped from job to job until he located this manufacturing job where he would receive tasks that could be completed without social interaction with others. Andy made a sufficient income to rent a studio apartment where he would spend all of his leisure time alone. He had no friends, acquaintances, or sexual partners; however, Andy was the most content in this world.

Andy is afflicted with schizoid personality disorder.

The American Psychiatric Association recognizes "the essential feature of the schizoid personality disorder is a pervasive pattern of detachment from social settings and a restricted range of expression of emotions in interpersonal settings" (DSM-TR-IV, 2000, p. 694). The APA continues by specifically delineating the diagnostic criteria:

A pervasive pattern of detachment from social settings and a restricted range of expression of emotions in interpersonal settings, beginning by early adulthood and present in a variety of contexts, as indicated by four (or more) of the following:

1. neither desires nor enjoys close relationships, including being a part of family
2. almost always chooses solitary activities
3. has little, if any, interest in having sexual experiences with another person
4. takes pleasure in few, if any, activities
5. lacks close friends or confidants other than first-degree relatives
6. appears indifferent to the praise or criticism of others
7. shows emotional coldness, detachment, or flattened affectivity. (p. 697)

The disorder usually begins to manifest in early adulthood and is found in many different contexts. It is relatively uncommon and may be difficult to diagnose because of the similarities in symptoms of other disorders. Further, the disorder is difficult to diagnose because the afflicted person does not display distress over the characteristic symptoms, rather they find them comfortable.

Neither Desires nor Enjoys Close Relationships, Including Being Part of a Family

Persons afflicted with schizoid personality disorder find no interest in initiating, developing, and maintaining close relationships. It is not uncommon for these persons to lack the interest or desire to be considered part of their biological family. They do not find membership in formal and informal social groups as particularly interesting or desirable and actively avoid social gatherings.

Almost Always Chooses Solitary Activities

Persons afflicted with schizoid personality disorder appear as introverted, but not shy. They prefer their own company to the presence of others. They are truly loners and are not distressed by their interest in being alone. This may be the defining characteristic of the disorder. They choose isolation because they find it pleasurable. They are not escaping a world that they perceive as threatening or anxiety producing. They just do not find others in the world particularly interesting. They are content to live in total isolation from others.

Has Little, if any, Interest in Having Sexual Experiences with Another Person

They do not desire sexual intimacy with another person, and what little sexual activity they find pleasurable is self-erotic. It is difficult to ascertain if the acts of self-arousal and sexual gratification involve fantasy over other persons.

Takes Pleasure in Few, if any, Activities

Persons afflicted with schizoid personality disorder have few activities in which they find pleasure. Those activities in which they do engage are solitary and generally appear to be obsessive. The activities are not physical in nature and are usually passive; listening to music through headphones for hours, playing chess in competition with computer software, or completing crossword puzzles one after another.

Lacks Close Friends or Confidants Other Than First-Degree Relatives

With exception of a sibling or a cousin, they have no friends or acquaintances. This characteristic also separates the afflicted person from others who may enjoy the presence of others of close interests and hobbies. Adolescent and young male adults who do not participate in athletic activities, are of above average intelligence, and are not considered part of the social mainstream commonly "find each other" and develop close relationships. They enjoy common interest in intellectual activities: debate, theater, and chess clubs, as well as board and computer games: Dungeons and Dragons. These social relationships are critical to the development and maintaining of healthy self-worth. They do not need to play football or hockey to find self-worth. They find acceptance and appreciation in the intellectual relationships with similar persons.

In contrast, while the person afflicted with schizoid personality disorder may find pleasure in the same activities and hobbies, he has no interest in the requisite social interaction and intentionally avoids it. He is truly a loner.

Appears Indifferent to the Praise or Criticism of Others

The person afflicted with schizoid personality disorder presents an egocentricity that is immune to the praise, criticism, or opinions of others. It is obvious; he just does not care about what others think of him. Praise for receiving exceptionally high scores on college entrance exams is not relevant to him. The scores may be relevant to him, but the praise he receives from others about his scores is irrelevant. His indifference to the opinions of others is even greater in situations of criticism. Simply, he is not concerned about what you think of him. It is irrelevant.

Shows Emotional Coldness, Detachment, or Flattened Affectivity

The person afflicted with schizoid personality disorder appears to walk through life without expression. He shows neither joy nor sorrow. He presents a bland or blank expression to the world. It is this criterion that is often misinterpreted. Persons afflicted with schizophrenia, autism, and serious substance abuse often present the same characteristic bland or blank expression.

Etiology and Course

Due to the small prevalence of this disorder, little is known regarding its origin. However, children and adolescents growing up in an environment with a first-degree biological relative diagnosed with schizoid personality disorder have a higher predisposition to develop the disorder. Consequently, this suggests the potential for inheritability or the influence of modeled behavior.

Persons afflicted with schizoid personality disorder commonly do not seek treatment, but are referred by family members. The afflicted person is generally not receptive to therapeutic interventions as he does not see himself as disturbed and he is not experiencing distress. He finds comfort in his lifestyle and discomfort in any attempts to change him from his authentic self. Basically, he sees the problem in the family members for their failure to accept him for who he is. He is not only reluctant to change; he is resistant. "It's your problem, not mine. Love me the way I am and leave me alone" is the verbal definition of his behavioral manifestation.

CHAPTER 4

Schizotypal Personality Disorder

SCHIZOTYPAL PERSONALITY DISORDER SCENARIO

Even the hallowed halls of the prestigious business school could not deter the muffled laughter of the graduate students as Joe entered the finance lecture class. Joe was peculiar. He arrived 5 minutes into the lecture. The presiding senior professor was not amused by Joe's lack of timeliness or his appearance and conduct that had distracted the entire class. Oblivious to the muttered laughter and the professor's stern glare, Joe walked to the front center of the lecture hall and plopped down on the seat. Still oblivious of his distraction, Joe noisily unpacked his laptop and following the loud musical introduction to the laptop's operating system, Joe looked up at the professor and waited for the lecture to begin.

This was typical of Joe's behavior and despite his obvious high intelligence, people looked at him in amazement. Others referred to him as strange, weird, and eccentric. His appearance drew immediate attention to him. His clothing was always mismatched, inappropriate for the setting, and unkempt. He rarely brushed his hair and was not attentive to the details of hygiene. While the other students were clad in jeans and sports shirts, he would dress in a sport coat, a wildly colorful tie, an extremely wrinkled and soiled white shirt, trousers that did not complement his sport coat, and red basketball shoes. In contrast, he would attend faculty receptions for the graduate students in bib overalls, T-shirt, and sandals with no socks. The faculty, students, and their spouses were appropriately dressed in business formal clothing.

Despite Joe's high-level intelligence, he adamantly believed in the paranormal. He firmly believed that he possessed a "sixth sense" that allowed him to not only predict the future, but also cause a change in someone else's future behavior. He was constantly telling others of his "special" skills. He indicated that he possessed these extraordinary skills since childhood and had been talking about them to anyone who would give him the courtesy to listen. This behavior continued throughout the first semester and by the beginning of second semester it was obvious to all, but Joe, that he was alienated from the others.

Typical of a new graduate school cohort, the students developed a social network off campus. Coffee-break colleagueship eventually turned into Friday afternoons at the tavern and the professors would also join in on the fellowship. Joe's presence was obvious, and, while the faculty and students discussed political issues pertaining to Economics, his conversations pertained to his paranormal skills. He would constantly tell his peers that he knew ahead of time of an event that affected someone. He informed others that he predicted hurricane Katrina, but that political officials would not return his phone messages. He was trying to warn them about the pending disaster.

Joe arrived at the tavern on the first Friday of second semester, but he was the only one in attendance. The next week the students avoided him and he did not have the opportunity to inquire about Friday's usual activity. He arrived on the second Friday, only to be alone. He made a point of asking a student at the following Monday's class and was informed that the location had changed and they thought all of the students had been informed. Joe arrived at the new location on the third Friday only to be alone. They had changed the location again and had not informed him.

Joe's suspicion was not a delusion; they were avoiding him. Joe's natural state of suspiciousness was reinforced. He was confident that students talking together were talking and laughing about him. Joe was confident that the experiences of high school and his undergraduate education would not follow him to this prestigious graduate school. Once again, Joe could not establish close friendships. The other graduate students remained cordial, but were unwilling to even share their leisure lunchtime with him, even though they spent most of their leisure time with other graduate students. Joe's anxiety increased. He believed that the others were plotting against him. Joe attempted to separate his academic life from his personal life and initiated a search to find a group of undergraduates that would appreciate his special powers. His appearance and conduct became more eccentric.

Joe was able to identify a group of undergraduates that accepted his social advances and welcomed his special skills and discussions of the paranormal. These undergraduates were off-mainstream members of the university drug culture. They would invite Joe to join them while they smoked marijuana and experimented with hallucinogens. It was great fun to bait Joe into demonstrations of his special skills. Joe was their "pet monkey," entertaining. It took awhile for Joe to recognize the reality of his significance to the group. Joe acknowledged his role with the group and his anxiety and paranoid ideations increased.

Joe hid from the world, showing little or no affect, and oblivious to the environment. Joe is afflicted with schizotypal personality disorder.

The American Psychiatric Association indicates that "the essential feature of schizotypal personality disorder is a pervasive pattern of social and interpersonal deficits marked by acute discomfort with, and reduced capacity for, close relationships as well as cognitive or perceptual distortions and eccentricities of behavior" (DSM-IV-TR, 2000, p. 697). The APA further delineates the diagnostic criteria for schizotypal personality disorder as following:

A pervasive pattern of social and interpersonal deficits marked by acute discomfort with, and reduced capacity for, close relationships as well as by cognitive or perceptual distortions and eccentricities of behavior, beginning by early adulthood and present in a variety of contexts, as indicated by five (or more) of the following:

1. ideas of reference (excluding delusions of reference)
2. odd beliefs or magical thinking that influences behavior and is inconsistent with sub-cultural norms (e.g., superstitiousness, belief in clairvoyance, telepathy, or "sixth sense"; in children and adolescents, bizarre fantasies or preoccupations)
3. unusual perceptual experiences, including bodily illusions
4. odd thinking and speech (e.g., vague, circumstantial, metaphorical, overelaborate, or stereotyped)
5. suspiciousness or paranoid ideation
6. inappropriate or constricted affect
7. behavior or appearance that is odd, eccentric, or peculiar
8. lack of close friends or confidants other than first-degree relatives
9. excessive social anxiety that does not diminish with familiarity and tends to be associated with paranoid fears rather than negative judgments about self. (p. 701)

Contingent upon the severity of the symptoms, it is commonly difficult to differentiate the diagnostic criteria for schizotypal personality disorder and schizophrenia. Indicative of this difficulty in diagnosing is that while the course of the schizotypal personality disorder is relatively stable, there is a higher probability of the development of schizophrenia from this personality disorder than others.

Ideas of Reference (Excluding Delusions of Reference)

Persons afflicted with schizotypal personality disorder view events as having meaning that appears unusual to others. They inaccurately interpret events in a fashion that is unique to them and is completely different from others that have experienced the same event; however, this interpretation is not based in delusion.

Odd Beliefs or Magical Thinking that Influences Behavior and is Inconsistent with Subcultural Norms (e.g., Superstitiousness, Belief in Clairvoyance, Telepathy, or "Sixth Sense" in Children and Adolescents, Bizarre Fantasies or Preoccupations)

Examination of this criterion assists in understanding the previous criterion; *ideas of reference.* Persons afflicted with schizotypal appraise themselves with paranormal abilities. They are not playing "parlor games," but truly believe that they possess special powers that influence their behavior. They believe that they have the ability to predict events. Following an event, they inform others that they predicted that it would happen. They often believe that they have the ability to influence another's behavior. Following an event experienced by another, the afflicted person may inform them that they made the event take place. If a coworker receives a promotion, the afflicted person may indicate that they were responsible for making this happen. They specifically indicate that they did not talk to the employer and praised the other's work, but rather sent a telepathic message to the employer, advising them to make the promotion decision.

Obviously these behaviors are viewed as eccentric and odd and seriously strain social and work-related relationships. Predicting future events, informing others that they predicted a particular event, and claims of extra-sensory perception are viewed by others as strange behaviors and they avoid contact and communication with the afflicted person.

The American Psychiatric Association is quick to indicate that these behaviors must be examined in light of the subcultural norms of the person presenting them. Persons of some ethnic and religious cultures, such as voodoo, occult, and Native Americans, for example, believe in their ability to predict the future, cause events to occur, speak in tongues, healing by the laying on of hands, and have "out of body experiences."

Persons may be modeling behavior that is expected in the subculture and may be under drug influence. Consequently, a diagnosis of schizotypal personality disorder requires an analysis of cultural beliefs and norms.

Unusual Perceptual Experiences, Including Bodily Illusions

Persons afflicted with schizotypal personality disorder may present symptoms that appear to be hallucinations; which further demonstrates the difficulty in differentiating the disorder from schizophrenia. They may believe that there is another person present in the room although it is clearly evident to others that there is no one else present. They may indicate that they hear a person whispering their name. In recognition of their belief in magical powers, they may actually believe the event is happening and is not a hallucination. They may believe they have the ability to communicate with deceased persons.

One must contemplate the diagnosis of schizotypal personality disorder with persons claiming to be fortune-tellers, palm readers, tarot card readers, and clairvoyants. Are they afflicted with schizotypal personality disorder, schizophrenia, modeling subcultural beliefs and expectations, or cleverly faking these abilities to turn a profit?

Odd Thinking and Speech (e.g., Vague, Circumstantial, Metaphorical, Overelaborate, or Stereotyped)

Persons afflicted with schizotypal personality disorder may present odd thinking and speech. The American Psychiatric Association indicates that one of the characteristic symptoms of schizophrenia is "disorganized speech (e.g., frequent derailment or incoherence) (DSM-IV-TR, 2000, p. 312). A person afflicted with schizoptyal personality disorder may speak in mannerisms not expected for the situation, but are focused on the issue and not incoherent. They just seem to express themselves differently than others. They may quote a poem, song lyric, or discuss a movie theme as an analogy to explain their view of the event, engage into a philosophical discussion over a pragmatic situation, or talk as if "thinking out loud."

These thinking patterns and speech make them appear odd or eccentric to others and, consequently, acquaintances and coworkers avoid engaging them whenever possible.

Suspiciousness or Paranoid Ideation

Persons afflicted with schizotypal personality disorder are cognizant that others are avoiding them, but have difficulty in understanding why.

Consequently, they develop paranoid ideations when they observe a group of coworkers gathered around the coffee pot in the break-room laughing. They believe that these coworkers are making derogatory comments about them and may be conspiring against them. When the afflicted person hears that his acquaintances have enjoyed social activity without his being invited to participate, he is suspicious of the nature of their activity without him.

In reality, the odd and eccentric behavior that they present does in fact precipitate alienation from others. The others are probably not conspiring against him, they just aggregately concur that work and social activities are much more enjoyable without him present.

Inappropriate or Constricted Affect

Persons afflicted with schizotypal personality disorder are typically socially inept. The characteristic symptoms of the disorder reduce their ability to respond appropriately, and consequently, having little successful experience in gatherings with others, they experience increased anxiety and the resulting speech and behavior is inappropriate for the situation. This increases others' perceptions of him being odd and eccentric, increases their interest in avoiding him, and reinforces his belief that he is different from others, but cannot understand why.

Behavior or Appearance that is Odd, Eccentric, or Peculiar

Persons afflicted with schizotypal personality disorder also present odd, eccentric, and peculiar appearance and behavior. Again it is significant to examine the person's behavior and appearance in relationship to their subcultural norms. Many adolescents and young adults tend to join groups that are out of mainstream life and they utilize appearance to demonstrate their disrespect of conformity. The "hippie" culture of the 1960s represented the then young adults' contempt for mainstream society and their unwillingness to conform. Those "hippies" of the 1960s are the "baby boomers" and the captains of industry and politicians of the twenty-first century. These eccentric young adults were not afflicted with schizotypal personality disorder, but rather were presenting the normative behavior of their subculture. One must, similarly, examine those persons presenting odd, eccentric, and peculiar appearance and behavior in every generation.

The "groupies" or fans of Marilyn Manson wear completely black clothing, dye their hair, paint their fingernails, and wear black lipstick.

Are these adolescents and young adults of the first decade of the twenty-first century afflicted with schizotypal personality disorder? No, they are demonstrating the normative behavior of their subculture.

Consequently, it is the individual whose appearance and behavior that is odd, eccentric, and out of place with their work and social peers that is subject to analysis.

The schizotypal disordered person may wear ill-fitting, dirty, wrinkled shirts to the workplace. His clothing will also be inappropriate in relationship to his peers' appearance in the social world. He may wear red tennis shoes with his wrinkled suit to a wedding, or striped tie with a bold-checked shirt and checked trousers of a different color and pattern. On the opposite hand, he may show up at the local theater to watch an afternoon movie in a tuxedo. His hair is not combed, he may have body odor from a lack of bathing, and fails to medically address his acne infected face.

His behavior is also socially inappropriate. He may pass intestinal gas in the presence of others and wildly laugh at his behavior. He may pick his nose, scratch his buttocks, or fondle his genitals in the middle of a business meeting. All in all, his appearance and behavior is odd and eccentric. Others find him rude, offensive, and "weird." Interestingly, he does not understand why others avoid him.

Lack of Close Friends or Confidants Other Than First-Degree Relatives

It is easily understood why the person afflicted with schizotypal personality disorder have few friends and acquaintances, other than first-degree relatives. Their behavior, appearance, and strange ideas of reference and beliefs are offensive to others. There are circumstances when a group of persons afflicted with schizotypal personality disorder form a social group. Hollywood movies "The Nerds" and the "Revenge of the Nerds" are examples of eccentric persons forming a social bond.

Excessive Social Anxiety that Does Not Diminish with Familiarity and Tends to be Associated with Paranoid Fears Rather Than Negative Judgments About Self

The person afflicted with schizotypal personality disorder is cognizant that others avoid him, but is not cognizant of why. This avoidance from others precipitates increased anxiety over time and as familiarity increases. One expects social anxiety to decrease with familiarity, but this is not the case with persons afflicted with schizotypal personality disorder.

This increase in anxiety precipitates paranoid ideations. Rather than examining one's self to determine the source of others' avoidance, they believe that the others are conspiring against them. Due to the inability of self-introspection, the afflicted person withdraws deeper and isolates himself. He actively disenfranchises himself by failing to examine himself in relationship to the negative judgments.

Etiology and Course

The American Psychiatric Association reports that "schizotypal personality disorder appears to aggregate in families and is more prevalent among first-degree biological relatives of individuals with schizophrenia than among the general population" (p. 699). Given the similarities in symptoms, sans the hallucinations and distortions of reality of schizophrenia and schizotypal personality disorder, one must consider the probability of learned behavior. A child raised by a schizophrenic parent has a greater probability of developing schizotypal personality disorder than a child raised in a home without a mentally ill parent. The child observes and emulates the behavior of the schizophrenic parent. It is also highly probable that the schizophrenic parent encourages the development of the "magical" paranormal belief, because the parent believes that the child possesses the paranormal skills.

Contemplate the number of evangelistic children with the alleged ability to heal by the laying on of hands. The child who is raised by a schizophrenic parent is informed that he possesses special powers to predict and change the future. Reinforcing their child to believe that possesses paranormal skills also reinforces the schizophrenic parent's delusion that their child possesses such skills. The modeled behavior and reinforced belief predisposes the child to develop schizotypal personality disorder.

Successful therapeutic intervention with persons afflicted with schizotypical personality disorder is rare and often contraindicated.

CHAPTER 5

Conduct Disorder

CONDUCT DISORDER—CHILDHOOD-ONSET TYPE SCENARIO

Tom is 9 years old and in the third grade. He is a year older than his classmates as he was held back in first grade because of immature and aggressive behavior. The extra year increased his maturity; however, his behavior also increased in aggressiveness. It was less obvious. His maturity also included the recognition that his acting out behavior in the presence of teachers, parents, and other adults resulted in varied levels of punishment—from restrictions to beatings. Tom realized that he could accomplish his objectives without using acting out behavior.

Prior to this acknowledgment, he would follow his emotions with impulsive, irrational behavior. If he was angry at another child, he would strike him. If he disapproved of his mother's "grounding" restriction on him, he would go out anyway. If a teacher would rebuke him, he would stand his ground and refuse to obey. These behaviors were self-defeating. The punishment would increase in duration and intensity. It was not until his father smacked him across the face for his bold defiance that he realized that there was more than one way to accomplish his goals. Rather than waiting until he was old enough and big enough to retaliate, he would become more covert in his behavior.

Tom firmly believed that the "only" person he could trust was himself and the feelings of others were absolutely insignificant to him. He could care less if someone's mother had died of cancer or their brother had been killed in Iraq. It made no difference to him. In fact, Tom secretly wished his mother would die from cancer and that his father would be deployed to Iraq. Tom was above average intelligence and used the intelligence and egocentricity to his favor. Tom no longer coveted others' possessions; he figured out ways to get his own and destroy those of others. Tom decided he would never be in second place to anyone. He believed that he was smarter than anyone else, including the adults who were continually harassing him.

Tom built a social network around him. He utilized his superior intelligence and his ferocity to command the network. Tom demonstrated his ferocity by either severely beating up a smaller youth or using a weapon to beat an older kid. Few demonstrations were necessary. Tom's reputation preceded him. He even initiated a rumor that he had ready access to a firearm and was prepared and anxious to use it. Tom had set up his own "goon squad" enforcers. Older and bigger kids with limited intelligence were his "lieutenants." Tom never had to commit strong-arm robbery to obtain kids' spending money, his lieutenants committed it for him and Tom would share the bounty with them. Tom also learned to ply his trade outside of the realm of the school building and playground. The public playground was his turf and when the kids refused to frequent the location, he would hunt them down and extort them. Tom was also smart enough to tell other youths that if they told anyone then he would retrieve his gun and kill them.

Tom's reputation for fierce brutality was a reality in the neighborhood. No one questioned his authority or "squealed" to a parent or teacher.

School was a drama for Tom. He tried to control his cockiness to no avail. He could not summon enough maturity to sit there quietly and be reprimanded in front of his peers. He was expelled twice for telling a teacher to "stick it where the sun doesn't shine." Tom learned his lesson well. You couldn't talk back to a teacher and get away with it. Tom learned to retaliate in a more covert manner. Two days after the last altercation, the teacher arrived at the parking lot to find a flat tire on the car. A puncture in the tread; probably caused by a nail. No, it was Tom's ice pick.

Tom could always circumvent his parent's groundings. He would simply wait till they were sound asleep and he would crawl out of the window. Unfortunately, Tom's lieutenants were not able to escape their homes at night, and rather than being alone, Tom started to hang out with the neighborhood street gang. It was not an easy start for Tom. They pushed him around and called him names. Tom finally had enough and assaulted the smallest member of the gang. Tom was beaten up by the gang members, but his tough ferocious attitude was clearly communicated to the gang's qualified members. Tom was adopted as a "wanna be," and he spent all of his free time with the members. He learned to smoke and drink, and he was taught how to handle a knife. The gang used Tom as a "runner," dropping off numbers and drugs.

Tom's intimacy with the gang was observed by the police as they conducted surveillance. In an attempt to cut off the flow of new members, the police contacted the principal of Tom's school. The principal met with Tom's parents and Tom's subsequent beating was the worst of his life. Tom was now under the close scrutiny of his parents and other adult relatives, the school officials, and the police. Tom had to modify his behavior to their expectations. They could make him modify his behavior, but not his egocentricity and attitude. Tom would become more secretive about his behavior.

Tom was still able to evade his parents at night and he would prowl the shadows looking for open windows to crawl through and steal money from purses and wallets. He would purchase his treasures and hide them in his room. He was also saving for a gun he could buy on the streets. When his level of frustration increased to the boiling point, he would displace his aggression. Tom began to delight in killing cats and dogs. Tom is afflicted with childhood-onset conduct disorder.

ADOLESCENT-ONSET CONDUCT DISORDER SCENARIO

Allen suffered miserably as a child and young adolescent. His father was a heavy hitting drunk. Allen cowered in the corner as he watched his father beat his mother. The combination of Friday and a paycheck resulted in a bender, and the combination of the drunkenness and the slightest innocuous comment resulted in the beatings. Allen, at 15, was ecstatic when his father was killed on the job.

His father's death opened a whole new world for Allen and his mother. The double indemnity life insurance policy and mortgage payoff propelled Allen and his mother from his father's imposed poverty. His mother bought new clothes and told Allen he could have whatever he wanted. His mother's feelings of guilt for her inability to protect him from his father motivated her to overindulge Allen. Allen could do no wrong and could do and have anything he wanted. It didn't take Allen long to realize this priority position and he exploited it. If he learned anything from his father, he learned to take anything you want, because nobody is going to give it to you. Allen determined that if his mother was so stupid to give it to him, he would take it all. Allen's ego grew in direct proportion to the indulgence. The transformation from poor abused kid to the pampered kid precipitated a significant change in Allen's personality.

Allen began to neglect his schoolwork and his grades plummeted. Allen discovered marijuana and enjoyed the mellow sensations of the high. Soon the marijuana turned to hashish, and the hashish turned to cocaine. His mother's financial indulgence was insufficient to cover his substance abuse. He was not physically addicted to drugs, just found it a pleasurable lifestyle. Allen turned to other activities to fund his pleasurable lifestyle.

Allen, despite his mother's attempts to control him, stayed out late, violating curfew every night. While prowling the streets, he would look for homes, cars, and businesses that he could illegally enter and steal from. He preferred cash, but in its absence, he would steal prescription drugs, firearms, and electronics that he could easily fence. During one breaking and entering of an occupied dwelling he awoke the resident and he was nearly apprehended. Occupied dwellings offered the greatest potential for a handsome score, but detection was extremely high. Allen stepped back to cars and unoccupied dwellings until he could bankroll enough money to purchase a handgun with a silencer from the local gunrunner.

The silenced handgun empowered Allen. Nothing stood in his way and he felt the rush as he entered an occupied dwelling. One night he killed a dog in an apartment while no one was home. He executed the dog just to enjoy the feel, the excitement. Allen thrived on the power that he possessed. He would never be detected, and if he was, he had no qualms about killing someone. In fact, he relished the thought of the prospect.

During one of his late night ventures, he looked through the window of a house to determine if it was worthy of entry. He observed a young woman asleep on the top of the bedcovers. The night was hot and humid and the house was not air-conditioned. The window was open and a small fan was blowing a cool breeze over her near nude body. Allen had an active sex life with young women to whom he provided cocaine, but the sex was always consensual. Allen became aroused at the thought of raping this young woman. The noisy fan in the room covered his entrance to the home. He stood in the dark next to her, and covered her mouth and at the same time he stuck the handgun against her face. Her scream was restricted and her fear was evident when she saw the handgun. Rather than taking the chance he might kill her, she, unwilling but without a fight, allowed Allen to rape her. As he left he told her that if she called the police he would come back and kill her. Allen laughed at her while she sobbed uncontrollably.

Allen is afflicted with adolescent-onset conduct disorder.

The American Psychiatric Association indicates that "The essential feature of conduct disorder is a repetitive and persistent pattern of behavior in which the basic rights of others or major age-appropriate societal norms or rules are violated" (DSM-IV-TR, 2000, p. 93). Conduct disorder is not classified as a personality disorder in the *Diagnostic and Statistical Manual of Mental Disorders*, Fourth Edition, Text Revised (DSM-IV-TR), but rather in the category of "Disorders Usually First Diagnosed in Infancy, Childhood, or Adolescence" (p. 13). It has been included in this book because of its close characteristic and diagnostic relationship with the antisocial personality disorder. The American Psychiatric Association specifies criterion 3 for a diagnosis of antisocial personality disorder as "there is evidence of Conduct Disorder with onset before age 15 years" (DSM-IV-TR, 2000, p. 706). Consequently, a diagnosis of antisocial personality disorder cannot be made without a previous diagnosis of conduct disorder.

The American Psychiatric Association provides extensive delineation of the diagnostic criteria for conduct disorder.

A. A repetitive and persistent pattern of behavior in which the basic rights of others or major age-appropriate societal norms or rules are violated, as manifested by the presence of three (or more) of the following criteria in the past 12 months, with at least one criterion present in the past 6 months:

Aggression to people and animals

1. often bullies, threatens, or intimidates others
2. often initiates physical fights
3. has used a weapon that can cause serious physical harm to others (e.g., a bat, brick, broken bottle, knife, gun)
4. has been physically cruel to people
5. has been physically cruel to animals
6. has stolen while confronting a victim (e.g., mugging, purse snatching, extortion, armed robbery)
7. has forced someone into sexual activity

Destruction of Property

8. has deliberately engaged in fire setting with the intention of causing serious damage
9. has deliberately destroyed others' property (other than by fire setting)

Deceitfulness of Theft

10. has broken into someone else's house, building, or car
11. often lies to obtain goods or favors or to avoid obligations (i.e., "cons" others)
12. has stolen items of nontrivial value without confronting a victim (e.g., shoplifting, but without breaking and entering; forgery)

Serious Violations of Rules

13. often stays out at night despite parental prohibitions, beginning before age 13 years
14. has run away from home overnight at least twice while living in parental or parental surrogate home (or once without returning for a lengthy period)
15. is often truant from school, beginning before age 13

B. The disturbance in behavior causes clinically significant impairment in social, academic, or occupational functioning.
C. If the individual is age 18 years or older, criteria are not met for antisocial personality disorder. (DSM-IV-TR, 2000, pp. 98–99)

Caveat

There is considerable controversy pertaining to the diagnosis of conduct disorder. Is conduct disorder a psychiatric condition, or a "set" of behaviors adopted by adolescents to adapt to their environment? The American Psychiatric Association acknowledges this controversy.

Concerns have been raised that the conduct disorder diagnosis may at times be misapplied to individuals in settings where patterns of undesirable behavior are sometimes viewed as protective (e.g., threatening, impoverished, high crime). Consistent with the DSM-IV definition of mental disorder, the conduct disorder diagnosis should be applied only when the behavior in question is symptomatic of an underlying dysfunction within the individual and not simply a reaction to the immediate social context. (p. 96)

This caveat or disclaimer does not help in ascertaining if an individual should be diagnosed with conduct disorder. Many of the behaviors delineated in the diagnostic criteria are behaviors common to all adolescents, some just more than others. The behaviors delineated in the entire subclassification of serious *Violations of Rules* are commonly "rights of passage" adolescent behaviors. What behaviors can be considered a function of adolescent development versus pathological?

This is an inquiry that must be addressed prior to any suggestion of a diagnosis. Further, the normal or expected behavioral manifestations exhibited by adolescents are relative to the individual's environment and perception of their environment. The variables that precipitate higher rates of crime in the urban environment also precipitate higher levels of conduct disorder like behaviors, but are youths accurately diagnosed with conduct disorder?

An adolescent growing up in a gang-infested neighborhood has few choices for survival and success. Youths who are not particularly athletic, highly intelligent, or large in stature have great difficulty in escaping the recruitment of the violent street gangs. Street gangs mark their neighborhoods by spray-painting gang graffiti logos on the back of stop signs, thus, designating their "turf." The gang aggressively recruits junior high school age youth. Unless the youth has strong support from family, school personnel, and nonaffiliated peers, gang involvement is requisite to survival. Intimidation to affiliate is not covert; it is obvious, aggressive, and dangerous. Failure to join may result in beatings, sexual assault of family members, and even death. Drive-by shootings are a way of life.

Unfortunately, gang affiliation also has a natural draw for some inner city youth. The gang offers the disenfranchised youth a new "family," complete with the physical signs of membership; gang specific colors, logos, gestures, and norms. The gang norms are dissimilar to societal norms; in fact, most are violations of the criminal code. There is also physical and economic security to gang membership. Nonaffiliation in a gang-dominated neighborhood leaves the youth at the mercy of the resident gang and also without protection from rival gangs. Gang membership provides a level of protection for oneself and family. Guns are readily available and the street reputation for "carrying" and wearing the "colors" is too strong for many youths to resist.

Neighborhood gangs also control the movement of illicit drugs, the numbers racket, prostitution, and neighborhood business security. Gang membership provides a source of income for the affiliated. Struggling in school, truancy is commonplace. Truancy results in confrontation with school officials and juvenile justice personnel. Dropping out of school and making a handsome tax-free income from gang-related illegal activities is a desirable alternative for many. Families, particularly single-parent mothers, may want their young males to stay away from gang affiliation but the increase in family revenue may be the difference between subsistence survival and some of the finer things of life. Youths who anxiously await their opportunity to affiliate are referred to as a "wanna be" and can be extremely dangerous. They have spent their days on the periphery of the activity, watching and learning.

Albert Bandura (1977), an internationally recognized developmental psychologist, suggests that it is not necessary for a youth to experience a behavior in order to learn it. Observing the behavior of the affiliated members, the "wanna be" learns the method of operation and appreciates the associated rewards or consequences. The youth learns that carrying a gun produces street respect, admiration, and economic rewards. Machismo rules the gang world. The tougher you are, the more respect and rewards you receive. Your income is directly related to violent aggressive behavior. The most violent and aggressive drive the most expensive cars; have the most spending cash and admiring young women. The draw to affiliate is overwhelming. The youth anxiously awaiting this rite of manhood are susceptible to behaviors that would be noticed by the affiliated membership. The junior high student who allows a teacher to berate him in front of others is a worthless gang member. However, the youth who retaliates by cutting or shooting the teacher is a rising young star and is initiated.

The danger lies with those who are fearful not to affiliate and consequently adopt delinquent criminal behaviors to adapt to the violent environment. Learning to assault before being assaulted, or carrying a weapon for self-defense is a proactive behavior for survival. Youth with an inability or unwillingness to fight are victims. Fight or flight, are the only alternatives in the gang infested urban environment. Fleeing only works for so long before you are eventually caught and assaulted. The youth adopts conduct disorder behaviors to survive. Is a psychiatric diagnosis of conduct disorder appropriate? The youth merely exhibits the diagnostic criteria as an environmental defense mechanism.

If the youth moves to a different neighborhood where the conduct disorder behaviors are no longer required for daily survival, the youth, who discontinues the behavior, is not a conduct-disorder youth. The youth who continues to exhibit the same behaviors in a new neighborhood, where they are not necessary for survival, is accurately diagnosed with conduct disorder. Prior to the *in re Gault* (1967) decision by the U.S. Supreme Court which gave minors the same due process protections as adults, judges commonly gave youthful offenders a choice; enlist in the military or go to jail. Most young offenders chose military service over incarceration. Those youths who were truly conduct disordered ended up in military prisons, and the others, who found no need to rely on the conduct disorder behaviors to survive, were successful in the military. The implications of misdiagnosing a youth as conduct disordered disenfranchise the youth. He is labeled as incorrigible, delinquent, and therefore, dangerous. He is more apt to be placed under the jurisdiction of the juvenile justice system than receive deferred prosecution. Dozens of studies have demonstrated that the further a youth enters the juvenile-justice system, the more criminal he becomes. He is ostracized by noncriminal peers and from age-appropriate and lawful activity. He is forced to associate with others similarly labeled. Unfortunately, many of the others are appropriately diagnosed as conduct-disordered. They are violent and aggressive. The misdiagnosed youth becomes further disenfranchised and finds acceptance in his new peer group. His criminal behaviors increase in frequency and intensity because these behaviors are reinforced by the new peer group. He has finally found acceptance and success, and society is now sentenced with the addition of a new lifelong criminal, and eventual inmate.

Diagnostic Criteria

This author has interviewed and evaluated several thousand adolescents that have been diagnosed with conduct disorder (CD) and served as a sworn expert witness in a large number of criminal trials involving these youth. The author will utilize specific examples of behavior as exhibited by these youth in the presentation of the specific diagnostic criteria for the disorder.

Conduct disorder can be diagnosed with a childhood-onset type and an adolescent-onset type. The types are differentiated by the single variable that the child must exhibit one of the criteria prior to the age of 10 years and the adolescent type cannot have exhibited any of the criteria prior to the age of 10. Further, it is common for those youths who are diagnosed with the childhood–onset type to display the criteria in greater number and in greater severity.

Males and females are both afflicted with the disorder; however, rates for males are significantly higher. Male behaviors are also more serious than those of females. The author will utilize the male gender in this discussion, but asks the reader to be cognizant that the disorder and associated behaviors are also found in females.

Aggression to People and Animals

1. Often Bullies, Threatens, or Intimidates Others (p. 98). The CD child or adolescent is the neighborhood and playground bully. He is found in every school playground. He always finds smaller children to threaten or intimidate. If he can gain a following of others, which he usually can, he may pick on a youth of a similar size and rely on the backup of his comrades to reinforce his threatening behavior. He may also utilize one of his followers to do the assault for him. He does not require an issue to initiate his bullying behavior. He may tell the youth to give him his lunch or his lunch money and failing to do so will result in a beating. He may just tell another youth that he doesn't like the color of his hair, or an item of clothing he is wearing. He may just insinuate that the other youth was looking at him and he demands to know why.

The intent is not to acquire the money or other items, but rather to position himself as the "king" of the playground that everyone must fear. The bully's ego is reinforced and he does the behavior purely because it is pleasurable and he lacks any concern for the victim. The victim is merely a rung on his ladder of establishing his dominance. Younger children, particularly those smaller in stature, live in constant fear that today is the day the bully will extract his pound of flesh from them. Once a child succumbs to the behavior of the bully, he becomes a regular victim.

Bullying has recently come to the forefront of issues for elementary and secondary educators. Annually there are numerous cases where junior or senior high students commit suicide because they are victim to relentless bullying activity. Children and youths who are blessed with high intelligence, however, lack social skills, physical attractiveness, or athletic talents are subject to verbal humiliation, teasing, and physical threats. A Midwestern high school valedictorian with a full scholarship to a prestigious Ivy League University shot himself while sitting in his car in the school parking lot. The suicide happened just moments prior to commencement. He was wearing his cap, gown, and National Honor Society cords. His suicide note indicated that he could not deliver the valedictorian address because it only affirmed everyone's opinion that he was indeed the "nerd" that he had been called throughout high school. This is not a singular incident. It is commonplace.

Conduct-disordered youths lead the harassment and, unfortunately, many other youths, boys and girls, chime in and create a daily environment of humiliation for the victim. Victims are afraid to answer questions in class and afraid to report the bullying to school officials. Reporting the bully to school officials results in further harassment, or worse, a beating. Bullying behavior is readily obvious and school officials who deny its existence have their head in the sand or would rather just not deal with it.

Can bullying behavior be stopped? School officials can provide consequences for the bullying behavior; however, the bully just takes his bullying behavior outside of the school environment. Peers can stop the behavior of a bully. These peers are not followers, but rather other students who find the bully's behavior repulsive. There are numerous instances in which varsity athletes have initiated a vigilante movement to rid the school of the bullies. The athletes utilize their superior physical strength and numbers to intimidate and threaten the school bully. However, this vigilante movement merely transfers the bullying behavior from a bully to a new group wearing varsity jackets. School officials turn a blind eye to these vigilante movements. The new varsity bullies are not a source of problems in school, are commonly good students, and have the support of their coaches and the athletic director. No school official wants to expel the "star" quarterback for initiating a movement to rid the school of the "problem students."

Law enforcement officers and juvenile justice practitioners are also less apt to respond with negative consequences to the varsity athlete who stops the activity of the bully. In contrast, law enforcement and juvenile justice personnel readily respond to the assault behavior of the conduct-disordered youth.

2. *Often Initiates Physical Fights (p. 98).* Children and adolescents afflicted with CD commonly initiate fights. They are not defending themselves against aggressors; they are looking to start fights. They pick their victims, always someone less capable of defending himself. The bully also moves quickly and stealthily, striking the first blow without being provoked. The victims who have no idea that they are going to be struck are immediately at a disadvantage, suffering from the first punch. Unable to adequately defend themselves, they are beaten, commonly brutally. A very common behavior of the CD youth in an unprovoked fight is to strike one solid punch, and before the victim can recover the aggressor pulls the victims shirt or sweater over their head, effectively blinding them from subsequent punches. This is a not a fight, but rather a criminal assault which should be dealt with as such. The CD youth commits the behavior for two reasons: to advance his reputation as "tough," and secondly, because he finds great pleasure in beating the victim up.

3. *Has Used a Weapon That Can Cause Serious Physical Harm to Others (e.g., a Bat, Brick, Broken Bottle, Knife, Gun) (p. 98).* This criterion has become more commonplace in the last two decades and guns are the preferred weapon. Youth of the 1950s and 1960s utilized brass knuckles, wrapped rolls of coins in their closed fists, and knives as weapons, but the proliferation of handguns has thoroughly changed the weapons of choice. There is no second choice. Adolescents with conduct disorder carry guns. Metal detectors at school entrances were not initiated because of the Columbine School shooting, they have been utilized in gang-infested high schools for years prior.

Conduct-disordered youth carry guns to reinforce their perception of "machismo," to intimidate others, and to protect themselves against youth with greater prowess in a confrontation. Physical fights are rare in comparison to gunfights. A youth who carries a gun does so because he is willing and ready to use it. He will not rely on the intimacy of a fistfight or a knife fight, he will draw and use his gun. Gangs have also successfully acquired fully automatic weapons and utilize them in "drive-by" shootings at rival gang members as well as innocent bystanders.

Gang affiliation has increased the significance of this criterion. Gang initiation rights commonly require a "blood in" ritual in which two behaviors are common; the initiate must survive a beating at the hands of affiliated members, and secondly, an initiate must draw blood on a victim in order to gain affiliation. Assaults on innocent victims are common to initiation rights. There are hundreds of reported incidents of female shoppers assaulted by knife and razor wielding gang initiates as they are walking to their vehicles at the mall.

The bully who is receiving retaliatory action from a vigilante student group will arm himself and use the gun without reservation. He does not give up his objective of achieving "machismo" status, and carrying a gun enhances it. The vigilante group discontinues their retaliatory activity and ignores the bully. They are not the recipients of his bullying activity and choose not to face the gun he now carries.

4. Has Been Physically Cruel to People (p. 99). The child or adolescent afflicted with CD will intentionally be physically cruel to others. He will deliver pain to others for his own personal gratification. Sadistic behavior is not uncommon. In a fight, he will deliver more blows than necessary to "win" the altercation. He may intentionally kick the person to break ribs, or stomp on a hand to break fingers. He does this sadistic torturous behavior because he finds pleasure in doing so. It meets his intrinsic psychological needs.

He does not limit his physical cruelty to victims of a fight. He will be physically cruel to younger siblings and even weaker adults, such as his mother. He will pinch, pull hair, and put his younger siblings in an arm lock until they begin to cry from the physical pain. He has no empathy or concern for the welfare of his victim. He laughs as he releases them, demonstrating his joy in causing them pain.

5. Has Been Physically Cruel to Animals. This is a very early indicator of the development of conduct disorder. It is commonly displayed by childhood-onset type conduct disorder. It is a behavior that continues into adolescence even after the CD youth has transferred his aggression toward other persons. The cruelty to animals is readily observed and has many manifestations.

The cruelty is reactionary as well as premeditated. Children with CD will pick up a puppy or a kitten by the scruff of the neck and if it scratches or bites him, he will throw it against a wall, break its neck, or drop it and kick it across the room.

The premeditated cruelty demonstrates a higher level in pleasure achieved by the behavior. There are an infinite number of examples, but these few will provide the reader with insight to the cruel nature of the conduct disordered youth:

- Drowning a bag of kittens in a lake or throwing the bag out of the car on a busy highway
- Holding two cats and tying their tails together with a short rope
- Tying firecrackers on the tail of a cat

- Throwing a cat or small dog into a yard with a pit bull
- Poisoning the dog next door for excessive barking

6. Has Stolen While Confronting a Victim (e.g., Mugging, Purse Snatching, Extortion, Armed Robbery) (p. 99). The conduct-disordered adolescent engages in face-to-face confrontation with others while robbing them because he derives great personal gratification in seeing the victim's fear. This particular criterion is extremely dangerous. He is demonstrating his fearlessness to himself and others and this reinforces his perception of "machismo."

Breaking and entering an unoccupied dwelling does not have the "rush" associated with the physical confrontation. His goal is to create fear and terror in his victims. This meets his intrinsic psychological needs and is, in fact, more significant than the financial gain. His egocentricity allows him to ignore the possibility of detection, apprehension, and conviction. The gun in his waistband protects him from the unexpected response from his victim and also increases the terror the victim experiences.

7. Has Forced Someone into Sexual Activity (p. 99). This criterion is another excellent example of the lack of empathy and concern for others that is characteristic of conduct disorder. The conduct-disordered adolescent will force others into nonconsensual sexual activity. Unlike the entitlement that motivates the narcissistic personality disorder afflicted person, the youth with CD does it because he derives pleasure from the power and domination that he has over others. Recognizing that he also is predisposed to cruel and violent behavior, he will rely on physical assault to accomplish his sexual activity. He will also utilize a weapon to force the person into the sexual activity.

This criterion is similar in psychological nature to robbery while confronting the person. Obviously his victim can identify him, but he relies on his ability to produce such terror in the victim that they do not report the incident for fear of retaliation. The conduct-disordered youth derives more pleasure from the power, domination, and terror of the assault than he does from sexual gratification. The orgasm is momentary, but the remembrance of the victim's terror lingers much longer and the behaviors of his disorder are reinforced and strengthened.

A conduct disordered youth who escapes the consequences of committing rape becomes a serial rapist. The orgasm is pleasurable and the domination is addicting. His lack of empathy and concern for his victim empowers him to commit similar acts again and again until apprehended and convicted.

8. Has Deliberately Engaged in Fire Setting with the Intention of Causing Serious Damage (p. 99). There are a number of motivations to consider with this criterion. "Causing serious damage" can be examined from a number of circumstances. Arson, the deliberate setting of fires, is committed by youth and adults for a number of reasons. Some youths set fires because it is similar to a paraphilia. They experience recurrent, intense, sexual arousal over setting fires. These youths and adults are not afflicted with conduct disorder or antisocial personality disorder and are not considered in this criterion.

Persons afflicted with CD set fires to cause serious damage—physical and economic. Arson is utilized as a mechanism for retaliation. A conduct-disordered youth may set fire to the home of a teacher who confronted him in school. He may set fire to a store whose owner forced him to leave his store. He may set fire to the automobile of his ex-girlfriend's new boyfriend. These arsons serve the purpose of retribution without detection. There is great economic damage and the potential for physical damage should the home, store, or automobile be occupied. He delights in the economic damage and inconvenience that he has caused to occur and does not care if someone is injured in the fire. He has no empathy or concern for the victims; instead, he believes it is just-desserts.

Adolescents afflicted with CD also commit arson for profit. They engage in arson because they have accepted a contract to burn down a building for money. Individuals interested in collecting insurance on an arson-destroyed building commonly do not wish to do it themselves or further become implicated. Arson is big business and organized crime actively pursues youths to set fires. Youths accept these contracts for sizable sums of money. The contract is completed through many levels, therefore precluding the owner's implication. Youths recognize that if they are detected and apprehended, they will probably be charged as juveniles and will receive minimal incarceration. The contract is "sweetened" by an additional sum awaiting them upon release from detention if they do not implicate the contract holders. The contract silence is also reinforced with the threat of death if they do implicate others.

Youth also commit arson for "fun." For many years, the city of Detroit has experienced hundreds of fires of abandoned houses on "devil's night," or the night before Halloween. Gangs of youth roam the city setting hundreds of fires. This is also a common activity of conduct-disordered youth during periods of civil disorder and natural disasters as witnessed in New Orleans following Hurricane Katrina in 2005.

Finally, adolescents afflicted with conduct disorder commit arson to cover up other crimes or as a "distraction" of public safety personnel while they commit another crime. Homicides, home invasions, and larcenies from buildings are cleverly covered up by arson. Arson is generally utilized by conduct-disordered adolescents with higher levels of intelligence. The retribution is more covert, the plans are more sophisticated, and detection is significantly reduced.

9. *Has Deliberately Destroyed Others' Property (Other Than by Fire Setting) (p. 99).* Conduct-disordered children and youth destroy the personal property of others to cause discomfort to the victims. The motivation may be for retribution, rage, or jealously. The teacher who humiliates a youth in front of his peers may find his automobile tires slashed. The storeowner that tells a youth to get out may return the next day to find his glass storefront smashed with a brick.

The smug actions of the owner of a new Mercedes may find his antenna bent, the side panel scratched to the bare metal with a key, or spray painted. It is not beyond the conduct-disordered youth to destroy property of another that he covets for himself. Unable to earn a varsity jacket, he destroys those of others who did qualify for the varsity letter. The conduct-disordered youth has no empathy or concern for the feelings of his victims.

10. *Has Broken into Someone Else's House, Building, or Car (p. 99).* The conduct-disordered youth has no reservations about violating the rights of others by breaking and entering others' houses, buildings, and cars. Others' private property is insignificant to him. He is only concerned with what he can steal from inside the residence, building, or auto. There is an additional variable associated with the breaking and entering of an occupied dwelling that is dangerous for the victims. A general characteristic of all adolescents is impulsivity. Combining the impulsivity of adolescence with the "machismo" and lack of concern for others, the breaking and entering of an occupied dwelling creates an environment of danger. The conduct-disordered adolescent does not carefully pick the occupied dwelling to break and enter. He does not know or care if the owner is at home. Further, the potential for an encounter is exciting to the youth and the gun in his waistband offers him the protection he needs if a confrontation does occur. Many youths so afflicted desire the encounter and this heightened excitement is stimulating. Breaking and entering of an occupied residence is a homicide waiting to happen.

11. *Often Lies to Obtain Goods or Favors or to Avoid Obligations (i.e., "Cons" Others") (p. 99).* Pathological lying is a core characteristic of conduct disorder. The behavior is so common that afflicted children and youth lie even when it is to their advantage to tell the truth. The success of the lie is directly related to the intelligence, age, and maturity of the child or adolescent. The higher the level of intelligence, age, and maturity, the more sophisticated and elaborate the lie. Lies are simply

mistruths to excuse one's behavior or to acquire something that the person desires. Lying is also a general characteristic of non-conduct-disordered children and adolescents; it is the severity that differentiates the two.

12. Has Stolen Items of Nontrivial Value without Confronting a Victim (e.g., Shoplifting, but Without Breaking and Entering; Forgery) (p. 99). The severity of this criterion is directly related to intelligence, age, and maturity. Younger, less intelligent, and less mature adolescents will exercise little planning in their attempts to steal. They will not scrutinize the potential victim stores for security personnel or cameras. They do not develop elaborate plans. They are commonly apprehended.

Successful shoplifting and forgery are the tactics of the older, more mature, and higher intelligence adolescents afflicted with CD. These adolescents become so sophisticated in their trade that they take and fill orders from customers. They have elaborate plans to elude all forms of security. They "case" the potential victim stores. They know the type and presence of security. They watch and listen. They know the fake announcements: "Clean up needed on aisle 13," is actually an announcement to plainclothes security officers of a probable shoplifter at aisle 13 plus or minus the number of aisles. These plans become so elaborate that they send a decoy that looks suspicious in nature to a specific aisle, await the announcement, and from a distance observe the appearances of the plainclothes security officers. They also know the plus or minus from the announced aisle. They come back the next day with the decoy and set him a long distance from the location of the item to be shoplifted. They await the announcement, know the response time of the security officers, elusively shoplift the item, and exit the store at the only location without a monitor.

Adolescents who attempt forgery of currency are destined to spend time in a federal prison. The forgery of currency is an impossible activity and older, mature, and high intelligence conduct-disordered adolescents do not attempt it. However, they are very skilled in larceny by conversion. Upon the announcement that a "big name" musical group is touring, the highly intelligent adolescent initiates his plan. He arrives the minute the box office opens and buys two (seats together) of the most expensive tickets. He immediately goes to the nearest office supply store and purchases identical color and weight stock paper as the tickets. He then scans the two tickets into his computer and prints off dozens of pairs of counterfeit tickets. He travels to nearby high school and university campuses. He sells the tickets at different locations at 50 percent of the value, indicating that he cannot attend the concert. As soon as he sells the tickets, he leaves town with hundreds to thousands of dollars in his pocket. The concert date arrives and fifty people arrive to occupy the same two seats. They have all been "conned" by the intelligent mature adolescent with conduct disorder.

Serious Violations of Rules

13. Often Stays Out at Night, Despite Parental Prohibitions, Beginning Before 13 Years

14. Has Run Away from Home Overnight at least Twice while Living in Parental or Parental Surrogate Home (or Once Without Returning for a Lengthy Period)

15. Is Often Truant from School, Beginning Before 13 Years (p. 99). The American Psychiatric Association has chosen to identify these three criteria as characteristic of conduct disorder. These three criteria are also characteristic of adolescents and particularly those whose parents are abusive and neglectful. These three criteria do not qualify adolescents for a diagnosis of conduct disorder, only a diagnosis of adolescent. This is very significant. In reiteration of the opening paragraph of the diagnostic criteria for conduct disorder, "as manifested by three or more of the following criteria" (p. 98). Consequently, if a child or adolescent exhibits all of these three criteria, 13, 14, and 15, he qualifies for a diagnosis of conduct disorder.

These three criteria are consistently manifested by youth diagnosed as conduct disordered; however, the reverse correlation is not accurate. These behaviors are inherent to adolescent development. This author rejects the premise that these criteria constitute a diagnosis of conduct disorder. This author is confident that if all of the teenagers in the United States were surveyed, the greatest majority would admit to having committed at least one if not all three of these criteria.

These behaviors are not criminal in nature, but the other criteria are. These behaviors are commonly referred to as "status offenses." Most states' Probate Codes identify these behaviors as "delinquent," but are not included in the same state's Criminal Code. These behaviors are violations because of the youth's status as a "minor child." The age of "minor child" also differs from state to state. Consequently, if a youth performs these behaviors in one state he might qualify for a petition of "delinquency" and in a neighboring state, his age is considered adult, and he cannot be charged as a "delinquent."

The differences between criteria 1–12 and 13–15 are significant. Children and youth displaying behaviors fitting criteria 1–12 qualify for the diagnosis of conduct disorder and those only displaying behaviors fitting criteria 13–15 should only qualify for further evaluation.

Etiology and Course

The origin of conduct disorder was discussed in the *Caveat* section of this chapter. In reiteration, examination and evaluation are critical to an accurate psychiatric diagnosis of the disorder. The implications for misdiagnosis are significant to the youth. Disenfranchisement from mainstream adolescent activities is probable and involvement in criminal activity with older peers is commonplace. Youths who adopt CD like behaviors to survive and succeed in a hostile environment may adopt new nonantisocial behaviors when the environmental variables change. However, the youth misdiagnosed with conduct disorder, who relocates with his family to a less hostile and aggressive environment, carries with him the implications of the inaccurate diagnosis. The school record with the diagnosis attached as part of the permanent record is transferred to the new school district, and the new school personnel respond to the misdiagnosis in contrast to observed behavior patterns. He will be assigned to special-education classrooms for the severely emotionally or behaviorally impaired and perhaps even enrolled in a special school for behaviorally disordered youth. Rather than being mainstreamed, he is forced back into a hostile environment in which his school peers are accurately diagnosed as conduct disordered. The youth becomes further disillusioned and disenfranchised and he is highly predisposed to a life of criminal activity.

Some conduct-disorder diagnosed youth merely mature out of the behaviors. This corresponds with R.D. Hare's (1991) Maturation Retardation Hypothesis. The development of the brain is arrested during adolescence and in later adolescence it matures and the conduct-disorder behaviors subside. "Many individuals with Conduct Disorder, particularly those with Adolescent-Onset Type and those with fewer and milder symptoms, achieve adequate social and occupational adjustment as adults." (DSM-IV-TR, 2000, p. 97)

In contrast, the American Psychiatric Association indicates that "early onset predicts a worse prognosis and an increased risk in adult life for Antisocial Personality Disorder and Substance-Related Disorders. Individuals with Conduct Disorder are at risk for later Mood Disorders, Anxiety Disorders, Somatoform Disorders, and Substance-Related Disorders." (p. 97)

In closing one must contemplate the origin of the adult disorders as described in the previous paragraph. The inquiry is, "Which came first, the chicken or the egg?" or rather, is the youth, misdiagnosed with conduct disorder, highly predisposed to the development of the adult disorders due to the implications of the misdiagnosis as an adolescent?

CHAPTER 6

Antisocial Personality Disorder

ANTISOCIAL PERSONALITY DISORDER SCENARIO 1

The young woman did call the police, and Allen was apprehended, tried, and convicted of breaking and entering and of rape. Due to his age, Allen was sentenced under the youthful offenders sentencing guidelines to 8 years in prison. Following 6 months in the County Jail, Allen was turned over to the State Department of Corrections to serve his sentence. He was assigned to the State Reformatory for Youthful Offenders. The prison was designed as a medium security facility to accommodate 1,500 prisoners between 18 and 25 years of age. Typical of the minority overrepresentation plaguing the national criminal justice system, the population was composed of 60 percent African American inmates, far exceeding their 20 percent of the general population. This was certainly not advantageous to slight-in-stature, Caucasian Allen.

Allen finished his 2-week stay in reception and the battery of psychometric examinations uncovered his well-disguised, above-average intelligence as well as his lack of conscience. Allen was easily diagnosed with an Antisocial Personality Disorder, and would have been diagnosed as psychopathic or a sociopath by older clinicians. Allen had neither remorse for his actions nor empathy for his victims. Further, he was completely egocentric. If it felt good, he would do it. The world was his to do with as he pleased. He experienced no anxiety and certainly no guilt for his behavior. He walked out of reception with a "chip" on his shoulder and "damn you all" attitude.

His "reception" in the "yard" was less than he expected. He antici-pated that his reputation would precede him. It was a delusion. He was greeted by 1,500 inmates hungry for the new "fish." Within the next 24 hours he would have to decide whether to affiliate with a prison gang or be sodomized by numerous inmates from different gangs. He chose to affiliate with a Caucasian gang, only to be sodomized by their membership. It was obvious that life was a temporary condition "in-side" the walls and Allen adjusted accordingly. He fashioned knives from toothbrushes and bedsprings and left his mark. Allen would rather kill than be assaulted. He established an "inside" kingdom with violence and death at the center. He never regretted his actions. Further, he lost no sleep at night. He was feared by all for his lack of empathy, his fero-city, and his intrinsic need for ever-increasing levels of excitement. Allen reigned as the supreme commander of this "gladiator unit," and he feared no one.

Allen was paroled after 4 years for "good behavior." His behavior was certainly not "good" but his ability to manipulate the corrections' officers (CO) was unequaled. His high intelligence allowed him to ma-nipulate the CO's into personal discussions in which the CO's would divulge personal information; full names, addresses, and information about their families. Allen would utilize "outside the walls" contacts to find the CO's families and take photographs. Allen would show the photographs to the unsuspecting COs and he would have them in his pocket, fearful that their family was in jeopardy. Their anecdotal re-ports of Allen's conduct were exceptional. He was released as a model prisoner.

Upon release, Allen reported to his parole officer, informing him of his residence and employment. The parole officer's caseload was ex-traordinarily large and he spent all of his time chasing fugitives. Allen recognized this situation and played the role of an attentive and conform-ing ex-con. In reality, Allen was settling scores, and setting up new heists. The young woman, who testified against him, mysteriously disappeared. Armed with a list of less intelligent ex-cons, Allen arranged several scores. Allen used his prison-accrued knowledge and parlayed it into numerous big scores. Money was stolen and people were murdered. Allen lost no sleep over his activity and enjoyed the pleasure of his profit. Delu-sional that he was smarter than law enforcement, he became careless and was finally apprehended for a bank heist. Allen was convicted of multiple felonies and was sentenced to life imprisonment without the possibility of parole.

Allen is afflicted with Antisocial Personality Disorder.

ANTISOCIAL PERSONALITY DISORDER SCENARIO #2

Guilty-Keith's world crumbled around him. He listened awestruck while the judge thanked the jury for their service then turned to Keith and his high-paid counsel and set a sentencing date for 1 month later. Dressed in a $2,000 suit and $400 loafers, Keith looked out of place in handcuffs as his attorney pleaded with the judge to continue the bond and leave Keith in the community through the appeal process. The request was denied and Keith was detained in the federal lockup awaiting sentencing.

Keith was convicted on numerous counts of fraud, embezzlement, and theft. If required to serve the maximum on each count consecutively, Keith would be imprisoned for 60 years. Until that very moment, Keith was confident that he would be acquitted. Keith's history of unlawful conduct started in his late adolescence. Early on he recognized that he was superior in intelligence to his peers and could manipulate them into doing whatever he desired.

Keith was not a particularly serious offender during his high school and college years, but he always straddled the law. He was mature and intelligent enough to keep his conduct in check. He played the game well. He would stand his ground and could communicate his anger and willingness to injure others without demonstration. Keith manipulated the teachers and administrators while in school. He didn't skip classes nor was he considered a behavioral problem. On the other hand, he did not excel in school, maintaining just enough of a GPA to assure his admission to college.

He was cognizant of the offenses that drew attention and stayed away from them. He refused to sell or take drugs and only drank alcohol in moderation. He didn't drag race his car, drive after drinking, or modify his car's appearance to draw the attention of law enforcement. He didn't hang out on the street, sneak into bars while underage, or surround himself with a gang of hoodlums or loud and obnoxious fraternity guys. He was friendly with everyone, but no one really knew Keith. He had no confidants or close friends. He dated regularly, but had no steady girlfriends. His handsome and rugged good looks allowed him to date most girls that he desired. He maintained a healthy sex life with a variety of young women, often stringing on several at the same time. Keith would commonly travel to different colleges on the weekends and establish new identities that could keep several young women attentive and sexually consensual.

Keith was a pathological liar and was good at it. He utilized his different identities to set up cons throughout a network of different colleges and universities. One of his earliest scams generated great wealth for him. Keith would arrive at a college campus on a Friday evening and find the freshman dormitory. Utilizing a large mock-up of the State Driver's License, Keith would create illegal driver's licenses for $100 each. A student would pay his $100 upfront, stand in front of the mock driver's license, and Keith would photograph him with a digital camera, download the student's name, address, and a phony date of birth, print out the license, have the student sign, and seal it in plastic with a standardized backside of the license. The word would spread like wild fire. By Sunday morning, Keith was on the road with $10,000 in cash in his pocket. His first stop was at a local campground where he would burn his clothing and wig.

Staying one step ahead of the police was easy. He moved about the United States, hitting a new college in a new state every weekend. He eventually realized that he could do two colleges in a given state every week. Keith was only 19 years old and clearing nearly $20,000 per week. He continued his college education at his hometown university by taking distance classes on his laptop while staying at campgrounds in his minivan. He dutifully called his mother and checked his voicemail at his apartment from a distance. He even made sure to make the rounds to different female acquaintances to maintain the illusion of being on campus. Keith was the ultimate con man.

Keith tired of his road activity and longed to settle down. Utilizing his advanced computer skills, Keith produced a false diploma from the largest state university and an employment history from a distant state. He developed a plan to embezzle funds from retired senior citizens. Keith researched the Internet for retirement communities with middle-class populations. He located hundreds of possibilities and carefully selected those communities where the population was in their 70s and 80s, rather than younger retirees. He wanted senior citizens that were more apt to be removed from the mainstream of economics, naïve, and vulnerable to the pitch of a handsome, gregarious, and charming young man.

Keith created a phony company that offered catastrophic health insurance which would step in and cover medical costs when expenses exceeded Medicare. This insurance would also cover nursing home expenses without the need to sell their homes and deplete their savings before assistance would kick in. Keith developed a flyer on his computer, printed off an original, and then made copies himself at the local office supply store. Utilizing a fake identity, Keith would rent the senior-citizen residential clubhouse for one evening, and then would hand-distribute the flyers to residences of the senior citizens. The distribution took place the same day of the seminar and free refreshments were provided.

Seniors would pack the clubhouse and Keith, looking and acting like the "perfect son," would give his Powerpoint presentation. Membership in this co-op health insurance program was limited and the closing date was nigh. The initial membership fee was $5,000, but annual dues were merely $25/month. The total initiation fee would be placed in an account to draw interest adequate to meet the group's catastrophic health needs in perpetuity. Keith had a number of examples to demonstrate the success of this cooperative program. It was not uncommon for Keith to leave these seminars with fifty or more $5,000 checks. Keith laundered the money through an offshore account within 24 hours. Keith's style of "hit and run" had generated a significant amount of cash, but it was time to change his con. Federal law enforcement could not be far behind.

Keith settled upon a plan to create a venture capital firm that was generating very high return on investments. Keith picked a wealthy community with a very high population of retired senior citizens. He carefully created his phony venture capital company. He created fake books utilizing legitimate corporations that had demonstrated remarkable profits. By combining these particular corporations he created a portfolio that was demonstrating remarkable returns on investments. It was an easy sell, because the portfolio utilized these successful stock exchange corporations. He recommended that persons should start by investing small amounts of capital to be safe. Within 6 months, Keith was sending out portfolio dividend checks that surpassed the returns that investors were experiencing with their brokerage firms. Consequently, the investors invested more and more funds and the dividends continued to pour in. No one was complaining; everyone was making money on their investments. Keith bought a home in the community, drove expensive cars, and dressed in $2,000 suits. He also donated significant amounts to local charities and received positive press for his altruism. The market crash of 2001 was unexpected and as the value of stocks plunged, Keith's investors demanded the sale of their stocks. There were no stocks to sell. Keith kept the money and used the steady flow of investments to return dividends to his investors. Keith lived the high style with the investor's money. The investors lost over $100 million.

Keith felt no remorse for those senior citizens that lost their entire savings. He only experienced anxiety over being caught.

Keith is afflicted with Antisocial Personality Disorder.

The American Psychiatric Association indicates that "the essential feature of the Antisocial Personality Disorder (ASPD) is a pervasive pattern of disregard for, and violation of, the rights of others that begins in childhood or early adolescence and continues into adulthood" (DSM-IV-TR,

2000, p. 702). This statement does not provide a clear picture of the potential severity and danger associated with the disorder. ASPD has also been referred to as Psychopathic Personality Disorder, Sociopathic Personality Disorder, and Dyssocial Personality Disorder. Regardless of the designated title of the disorder in previous editions of the Diagnostic and Statistical Manual of Mental Disorders, the general criteria have changed little.

The current American Psychiatric Publication, the *Diagnostic and Statistical Manual of Mental Disorders*, Fourth Edition, Text Revised (DSM-IV-TR), published in 2000, delineates the diagnostic criteria of the Antisocial Personality Disorder as follows:

A. There is a pervasive pattern of disregard for and violation of the rights of others occurring since age 15 years, as indicated by three (or more) of the following:

1. failure to conform to social norms with respect to lawful behaviors as indicated by repeatedly performing acts that are grounds for arrest
2. deceitfulness, as indicated by repeated lying, use of aliases, or conning others for personal profit and pleasure
3. impulsivity or failure to plan ahead
4. irritability and aggressiveness, as indicated by repeated physical fights or assaults
5. reckless disregard for safety of self or others
6. consistent irresponsibility, as indicated by repeated failure to sustain consistent work behavior or honor financial obligations
7. lack of remorse, as indicated by being indifferent to or rationalizing having hurt, mistreated, or stolen from another

B. The individual is at least 18 years of age
C. There is evidence of Conduct Disorder with onset before age 15 years
D. The occurrence of antisocial behavior is not exclusively during the course of Schizophrenia or a Manic Episode. (p. 706)

This diagnostic criteria identifies general areas of behavioral disorder, but does not provide a realistic picture of the varied behaviors on a continuum from less to more severe. The diagnosis, is significantly more prevalent in males than females, is chronic, and lifelong.

Failure to Conform to Social Norms with Respect to Lawful Behaviors as Indicated by Repeatedly Performing Acts that are Grounds for Arrest

This criterion indicates that persons afflicted with ASPD violate social norms and, specifically, behavior that is prohibited by the criminal code. The ASPD does not just violate social norms such as failing to wear shoes in a grocery store, smoking in smoking restricted areas, and public profanity, he performs behaviors that are significant violations of the criminal code. The ASPD may shoplift, break and enter households, assault with weapons, steal automobiles, and commit murder. Not all persons afflicted will commit all of these behaviors, but some will commit the most heinous of crimes. Infamous serial killers Ted Bundy, John Wayne Gacy, Kenneth Bianchi (Hillside Strangler), Jeffrey Dahmer, and numerous others were diagnosed with ASPD. The characteristics of the disorder allow if not empower them to do these heinous crimes.

There are also a significant number of persons with ASPD that commit economic crimes that affect the lives of millions of people. The same set of characteristics allows and empowers corporate executives and political officials, elected and appointed, to embezzle billions of dollars from taxpayers, stockholders, and employees. It is significant to acknowledge this perceived dichotomy in behavior. Serial rapists and murderers violently assault their victims and terrorize the citizenry. Corporate and political figures afflicted with the same diagnosis inflict horrendous chaos on the lives of millions. Agreed, the behaviors are different in relationship to the level of violence, but the blatant disregard for social norms and the law is the same. Thus, in reality, the victims of the embezzling ASPD far out number the victims of the violent ASPD.

This disparity in type of behavior cannot be ignored. The number of persons afflicted with ASPD that rape and murder are few in comparison to those who financially destroy the economic lives of millions of others. These covert behaviors must be readily acknowledged as dangerous. Corporate executives that "cook the books," steal millions of dollars, and force the bankruptcy of their corporation have stolen the life savings of their employees and stockholders. One must contemplate how many persons have suffered and died because of the loss of their jobs, homes, personal savings, investments, and pension programs.

This disorder cannot be reserved for those individuals who commit the heinous crimes that terrify the citizenry. It is not just those criminal behaviors that produce physical pain, injury, and death, but all of the behaviors designated by society as criminal. The salient feature of this criterion is not the violence of the behavior, but the blatant disregard for others. If ASPD is perceived by the public as only those who commit physically violent crime, then the smooth talking con man steals millions from unsuspecting victims. He is the "Wolf in Sheep's clothing" that successfully destroys the lives of millions.

It is analogous to the concept of "stranger-danger" that we teach our children. It is our intent to keep our children safe from sexual predators.

Ask any preschooler or early elementary schoolchild to describe the "dangerous stranger," and they will describe an ugly man dressed in dirty shabby clothing lurking in the bushes. So when a man dressed in a nice suit, driving a bright shiny new car, pulls up next to them on the sidewalk, rolls down the window, holds up a golden retriever puppy, and asks them if this is their puppy ("The puppy was in the street and I nearly ran it over with my car. Would you help me find which little boy/girl it belongs to?"), he is not perceived as a dangerous stranger by the child. The focus is on the puppy and the child is not alerted to the potential danger because the man dresses, talks, and drives a car like their grandfather.

Danger and violation of law comes in different packages and flavors. Ted Bundy was a handsome, intelligent, and articulate man. He was not ugly, dirty, or dressed in shabby clothing. He had been described as the boy next door and young women were readily attracted to his handsome looks and gregarious, courteous mannerisms. These young women who got into his vehicle would never have associated with an ugly, dirty man dressed in shabby clothing.

The level of intelligence of the person afflicted with ASPD is also reflected in the type of behaviors that they perform. Generally speaking, the higher the level of intelligence, the more covert the behavior, and in contrast, the lower the level of the intelligence of the person afflicted with ASPD, the more overt the behavior. The person with lower intelligence is more apt to commit armed robbery of a convenience store without considering the presence of a surveillance camera. He may commit a breaking and entry of a randomly selected occupied dwelling without reconnaissance and find himself facing an owner with a handgun or a pair of pit bull watch dogs. He may attempt a mugging in a well-lit parking lot frequently under the surveillance of cruising patrol cars. His actions are not well planned, his crime scenes chaotic, and consequently, his reactions unpredictable. Failing to reconnaissance the convenience store, he may find himself in a situation where the owner is armed and a gunfight ensues. Surprised in the act of breaking and entering, he may kill the owner. The man afflicted with ASPD and low intelligence is dangerous.

In contrast the man with ASPD with higher intelligence carefully plans out his criminal activity. He is rarely impulsive and usually successful. He is good at his trade. If his criminal activity requires physical activity, such as a burglary, his plan is premeditated. He is not random in his selection of residences. He is seeking a "big score" and conducts intensive investigation. He is fully aware of the potential prize, is aware of surveillance cameras, and enters at the most opportune time; that one in which he has the lowest probability of detection and the highest probability of success. This man will not engage in armed robberies of convenience or liquor stores, or attempt a mugging. He is discreet and covert. This is the same man that exploits others to complete his criminal activity; keeping himself as far removed from the crime as possible. He is also the ultimate con man.

Deceitfulness, as Indicated by Repeated Lying, Use of Aliases, or Conning Others for Personal Profit or Pleasure

This diagnostic criterion and the previous one are greatly influenced by the level of intelligence. Pathological lying is a general characteristic of ASPD, but intelligence reflects one's success in utilizing it for profit or pleasure. Persons with ASPD and low intelligence lie to cover up their actions or deceive others for obtaining money, drugs, sex, and other pleasurable activities. However, their lowered intelligence precipitates a lack of finesse and continuity and they are commonly caught in the lie. Many corrections officials have indicated that the only persons with ASPD in prison are the "stupid" ones. This not only reflects the poor planning or impulsivity of their criminal activity, but also their inability to maintain a consistent lie or malinger when under interrogation by criminal investigators.

In contrast, the highly intelligent person with ASPD is a very effective liar. Not only is he articulate in his deceitful propositions, but he also recognizes the significance of "appearance." The ASPD con man appears affluent, utilizes false credentials, and carefully selects his victim group. He generally preys upon the elderly, proposing investments with very attractive returns on their investments. Wealthy widows are particularly susceptible to this person. Many persons with ASPD also exhibit the characteristics of Narcissism. The combination of handsome looks, being articulate in the spoken and written word, charm, and attentiveness (with a disposition for pathological lying) is "too good to be true" to the wealthy, lonely widow. And it is too good to be true. They are the prey of this predator.

Impulsivity or Failure to Plan Ahead

This criterion is most commonly characteristic of the ASPD person with lower intelligence and/or the young. As indicated in previous discussions, their impulsivity and failure to plan result in a failed criminal activity, their conviction, and sentence to prison. As the ASPD person either matures or learns from the experiences associated with incarceration, they become more effective in the planning of their criminal activity, thus reducing the potential for apprehension. They change the type of crime they commit and are apt to work alone rather in gangs. Each additional collaborator in crime increases the probability of detection.

Irritability and Aggressiveness, as Indicated by Repeated Physical Fights or Assaults

This criterion, similar to the previous criteria, has differing levels of severity contingent upon the intelligence of the afflicted person. Irritability and aggression are common characteristics in all persons diagnosed with ASPD. It is the expression of these characteristics that differ.

The person with ASPD and lower intelligence overtly exhibits his irritability and aggressiveness through frequent confrontations with others. These confrontations may result in assaulting behavior and fights. This predisposition to be confrontational, when coupled with impulsivity, increases the probability of a physical fight. Lower intelligence and a lack of maturity indicate that the person's repertoire of behavioral responses is limited. When confronted by another person, his impulsivity and his lack of behavioral alternatives result in a physical confrontation. Being berated in front of his peers by a storeowner may result in his throwing a rock through the store window or assaulting the owner. Irritated and aggressive, he lashes out in anger without considering the consequences of his actions.

Inmates between the ages of 18 and 25 represent the majority of the U.S. prison population. Latent adolescence, unemployment, and impulsivity alone can account for much of this population; however, the characteristics of ASPD are readily apparent. Medium security prisons for these youthful offenders are nicknamed as "gladiator camps." These young, immature, and perhaps ASPD inmates are irritable and aggressive. Fights are commonplace every day. They lacked the maturity to keep themselves from being apprehended in the first place, and now they lack the maturity to keep themselves out of trouble while behind the walls. They fail to recognize that every time they fight time is added on to their early release date.

Reckless Disregard for the Safety of Self and Others

Persons afflicted with ASPD have an ever-increasing need for heightened stimulation. Coupled with impulsivity and disregard for social norms, these characteristics collide and precipitate an unsafe environment. Young street-dwelling persons with ASPD carry weapons. It is their demonstration of "macho" aggressiveness, and willingness to take care of business. The combination of ASPD and guns equates to one thing; death.

These same persons experiment with various drugs, drag race through the community, and are sexually promiscuous. They possess a delusional perspective that they are invincible. They believe that they will never be apprehended, never die in a gunfight, crash their vehicles, or contract AIDS. This perception of being all powerful is dangerous and leads to early death.

Consistent Irresponsibility, as Indicated by Repeated Failure to Sustain Consistent Work Behavior or Honor Financial Obligations

This characteristic is readily observed at the onset of the disorder. It is apparent in their inability to finish high school. The inability to attend school every day is an early demonstration of irresponsibility. If they haven't been expelled for gross misbehavior, they either just drop out or wait until they are expelled for truancy. This criterion is also apparent in the workplace. Initially, they have no interest in finding employment and when forced to take a job, they are usually fired for tardiness, absence, or lack of productivity.

Interestingly, many of these youthful men with ASPD are forced to find and maintain employment as a condition of probation or parole. They are fully cognizant that maintaining employment is a condition of release or in lieu of incarceration. The consequence is obvious. If they lose their job, they will go to jail or prison. This fact does not seem to influence their behavior and they continue to demonstrate their irresponsibility.

This criterion is also apparent in financial dealings, lawful and unlawful. If they are successful in finding someone to co-sign on a loan for a vehicle, they will not make the payments. Even if they have the money, either legally or illegally gained, they are more apt to spend the money on pleasurable activities or products, than make the loan payment. Ten thousand dollars in the pocket of a young man with ASPD is more apt to be spent on "top of the line" chrome wheels for their vehicle than the vehicle itself. It is a delusion that no one will repossess their vehicle. New clothes, drugs, and the high life drive their financial irresponsibility.

In reiteration of the last paragraph, court costs and fines are part of conditional release on probation for a criminal offense. The consequence is obvious; if one fails to pay their court costs or fines, he will go to jail or prison. Once again this consequence eludes them as they buy the "top of the line" chrome wheels.

Men afflicted with ASPD are notorious for failing to pay alimony and childcare ordered by the court. They walk away from their court ordered financial obligations. Over the course of the last 10 years, numerous states have passed legislation to incarcerate those men who fail to pay their childcare. These laws do not influence the irresponsible behavior of the men with ASPD. They worry about the incarceration after they are arrested and awaiting sentencing on contempt of court charges. Until that arresting officer arrives at their front door, they firmly believe that they won't get caught, convicted, and sentenced to prison.

Lack of Remorse, as Indicated by Being Indifferent to or Rationalizing Having Hurt, Mistreated, or Stolen from Another

This criterion is the most salient, severe, and potentially dangerous characteristic of the ASPD. Stating a lack of remorse slightly differently from the DSM-IV-TR, the ASPD is conscience-deficient. The person afflicted with ASPD does not feel sorry, bad, or remorseful over his behavior. He does not experience guilt for his injurious behavior to another. This deficiency in conscience empowers him to do what he pleases, and that is the guiding motivation. The man with ASPD only indulges in behaviors that are pleasurable to him and meet his intrinsic psychological needs. His total egocentricity dictates that the world is here for his pleasure and profit and all others are insignificant.

Acknowledging this criterion, one can begin to understand how a person can embezzle millions of dollars from others and not be bothered. We can begin to understand how a man can use date rape drugs to fulfill his sexual urges and needs. Understanding and approving are two entirely different things. It is through this understanding that guilty parties can be identified, apprehended, prosecuted, and sentenced.

The aggregate personality disorder is completed through this criterion. If a man with ASPD is intelligent, aggressive, and vindictive to his wife for divorcing him, he loses no sleep over having her "disappear" in a boating accident; no alimony and childcare to pay. If the "disappearance" happens before the filing of the divorce papers, he also saves on the attorney fees and collects on her life insurance. A man with ASPD could arrange for the death of his business partner before his partner discovers the embezzled funds, or he could just take his embezzled funds out of the Swiss Bank Account and move to a country that does not have an extradition agreement with the United States.

The schemes and severity do not have to be as grandiose as those presented:

Infidelity without guilt or remorse for either the spouse or the mistress

Stealing a thousand dollars a week off the restaurant receipts

Signing a bogus contract with half the money upfront to fix an elderly couple's roof

Starting a rumor that gets your neighbor fired from his job

Filing a false insurance claim

Slashing the tires of your college professor's car because he failed you,

Starting a rumor that your college professor is sexually involved with a student,

Stealing your infirmed parent's social security checks and not providing care for them.

All of the above are either violations of another person and/or a violation of law. The person with ASPD can do any of these and a million other activities without feeling guilt. Neither does he feel remorse or empathy for the person he has injured.

Etiology and Course

The American Psychiatric Association indicates that "Antisocial Personality Disorder is more common among the first-degree biological relatives of those with the disorder than among the general population" (DSM-IV-TR, 2000, p. 704). This statement implies that there is a genetic predisposition to develop ASPD. There is no definitive etiology of the disorder and researchers have suggested environmental as well as genetic factors that may be variables in its development.

R.D. Hare (1990), an internationally recognized authority on ASPD, conducted research examining the EEG patterns of adults diagnosed with the disorder. Hare postulated that the cerebral functioning of an adult diagnosed with ASPD was similar to that of normal adolescents. Hare compared the EEG patterns of normal adolescents with those of adults diagnosed with ASPD. His findings demonstrated similarities in the EEG patterns.

Hare concluded that the brains of adults diagnosed with ASPD were arrested during adolescence. Adolescence occurs at the time of puberty, at which time the brain grows to its full cellular capacity. Adults with ASPD experienced a developmental phenomena he titled "Maturation Retardation Hypothesis." This is not to be confused with clinical mental retardation, but rather, a portion of the brain is arrested, stopped, or slowed in development. Behaviors and characteristics common to both normal adolescents and adults with ASPD support Hare's theoretical perspective.

Researchers that suggest that the etiology of ASPD is environmental, support theoretical perspectives pertaining to nurture. Researchers suggest that ASPD develops from environments in which the child is severely abused and neglected. These children recognize that they cannot depend upon anyone to provide a safe haven. These children develop egocentricity as a defense mechanism to their hostile environment. They choose not to trust or rely on others for survival and success. Consequently, no one but themselves has worth. Their harmful behavior toward others is irrelevant, insignificant, and justifiable.

Researchers also suggest that overly pampered children are at risk to develop ASPD. Children develop an egocentricity heavily laden with entitlement when their inappropriate behavior is excused and natural consequences for these behaviors are prevented from occurring. These children believe they can do no wrong, in fact, they are bigger and better than the law. Parents who excuse their children's behavior by blaming it on institutions such as schools are doing their children a disservice. These children learn that they can do whatever they please and there are no consequences for their behavior.

Adolescents are prone to impulsivity, have difficulty in deferring gratification, are egocentric, irritable or moody, and irresponsible. These behaviors and characteristics are also common in the diagnostic criteria for the Antisocial Personality Disorder.

Antisocial Personality Disorder can be considered a flaw in the character that is chronic and lifelong; however, there is a decrease in the intensity and severity of the behaviors associated with age. As individuals grow older, the characteristic symptoms decrease in severity, intensity, and frequency.

The prospect for therapeutic intervention with ASPD is slim. The characteristics of the disorder preclude the person from change. The person with ASPD only changes behavior when finding the consequence for the behavior to be more severe than the pleasure derived from doing the behavior. The man with ASPD who commits rape and is not detected becomes a serial rapist. The pleasure derived from the rape reinforces the behavior and the failure of the system to provide any consequence reinforces the ASPD. However, should he be apprehended, prosecuted, and sentenced to prison for 20 years for the rape, he will reconsider the behavior of rape after he is paroled. That is, assuming the thought of returning to prison for 20 years is a deterrent.

CHAPTER 7

Borderline Personality Disorder

BORDERLINE PERSONALITY DISORDER SCENARIO

Tami paced the floor impatiently waiting for the phone to ring. Allison had promised to call her to go on a shopping spree. Tami looked at her watch and realized that Allison said she would call by 10 AM and it was now 10:08 AM. She mused whether Allison realized that she had better things to do than wait around for her call. Exasperated, Tami calls Allison's cellphone. As Allison answers the phone, Tami demands to know why she hasn't called. Allison, shocked by the abrupt and irate inquiry, apologizes and informs Tami that she was dropping her daughter off at the babysitter. Tami, realizing the impulsivity of her call and inquiry, quickly regroups and apologizes for being intrusive and indicates that she was worried that something had happened to Allison.

Tami's life is characterized by similar situations. Whenever Tami finds a new acquaintance, she grabs and holds on as if this person was going to escape. Tami cannot describe herself, unless it is in context with another person. Tami is someone's wife or someone's best friend. Tami has a long string of friends, acquaintances, lovers, and husbands. All have left her. As Tami characterizes herself as a part of someone else's life, she has no authentic perception of herself alone. Tami is incapable of being alone. She has no persona that defines her as an individual.

Tami's history of relationships is a pattern of intensity and then abandonment. Her fear of abandonment motivates all of her personal interactions; however, it is this fear that is exhibited in her behaviors that drive others away. Tami is either monopolizing the time of a friend or she is between friends and desperately seeking out a new one. When Tami identifies a new acquaintance, she moves in quickly to establish a commitment. She also perceives the friendship as more intimate than the other party and she sets herself up for failure. Tami not only monopolizes the leisure time of the new friend, but also exhibits jealousy if the friend talks with or goes out with someone other than her. When Tami hears of her "best" friend having lunch with someone else, she initiates an aggressive challenge that is offensive to all parties. She demands to know where they went, what they did, and why she wasn't included in the activity. Tami will not initiate the daily contact expecting the other party to do so in definition of her commitment to the relationship. When the other person does not call, she is furious and demanding. It is only a matter of time before the other person calls off the relationship and Tami is devastated.

Tami is either intensely monopolizing her lover/husband or without a lover/husband and looking for one. Her sexual relationships are as intense as her friendships. When Tami is between lovers, she is desperately seeking a new one and demonstrates impulsivity in the process. She searches through the singles bars, drinking excessively, and flirting with every available man. She demonstrates little judgment and is sexually promiscuous. In the sober state of the morning after, she realizes that it was a one-night stand and she has been abandoned again. This circumstance does not modify her approach to the problem or her behavior. Fearing the sense of loneliness, she repeats the pattern of behavior until she finds someone who stays more than just the night. If he calls the next day asking her out for dinner, Tami's impulsivity is demonstrated in her belief that this very brief encounter is going to be long-lasting. She grabs on as if there is no tomorrow. Tami believes that her new lover is as completely committed to the relationship as she is, but he must prove it to her. Tami demands that his total time be hers and that he will drop all other friendships, male, and particularly female. If he maintains his male friends, she is always complaining about how much time he spends with them, what were they doing, and making accusations of infidelity. Tami's demands on his time eventually drives him away and she is devastated.

Tami's initial response to his departure is one of intense anger characterized by screaming, swearing, and assaulting behavior. When she realizes that the anger pushed him even further away, she resorts to suicidal threats to get him to return. Tami's sense of worth and perception of self is destroyed again. Her sense of being unworthy is reinforced by the abandonment. Tami invariably experiences a bout of depression following the loss of the relationship, however, she will not learn from previous errors. Tami goes about business as usual, desperately looking for another close friend, lover, and husband.

Tami is afflicted with borderline personality disorder.

The American Psychiatric Association indicates "the essential feature of the borderline personality disorder is a pervasive pattern of instability of interpersonal relationships, self-image, and affects, and marked impulsivity that begins by early adulthood and is present in a variety of contexts" (DSM-IV-TR, 2000, TR, p. 706). Predominately a disorder diagnosed in females, the author will utilize the female gender in describing the diagnostic criteria. The American Psychiatric Association delineates the diagnostic criteria as follows:

A pervasive pattern of instability of interpersonal relationships, self-image, and affects, and marked impulsivity beginning by early adulthood and present in a variety of contexts, as indicated by five (or more) of the following:

1. frantic efforts to avoid real or imagined abandonment. Note: Do not include suicidal or self-mutilating behavior covered in Criterion 5
2. a pattern of unstable and intense interpersonal relationships characterized by alternating between extremes of idealization and devaluation
3. identity disturbance: markedly and persistently unstable self-image or sense of self
4. impulsivity in at least two areas that are potentially self-damaging (e.g., spending, sex, substance abuse, reckless driving, binge eating). Note: Do not include suicidal or self-mutilating behavior covered in Criterion 5
5. recurrent suicidal behavior, gestures, or threats, or self-mutilating behavior
6. affective instability due to a marked reactivity of mood (e.g., intense episodic dysphoria, irritability, or anxiety usually lasting a few hours and only rarely more than a few days)
7. Chronic feelings of emptiness
8. inappropriate, intense anger or difficulty controlling anger (e.g., frequent displays of temper, constant anger, recurrent physical fights)
9. transient, stress-related paranoid ideation or severe dissociative symptoms. (p. 710)

Frantic Efforts to Avoid Real or Imagined Abandonment

Persons afflicted with borderline personality disorder (BPD) are obsessed with the potential for rejection and abandonment. Their perception of the environment and persons' responses to them influence their feelings of self-worth and image. They misperceive circumstances as rejection. The girlfriend who calls to cancel a luncheon date and shopping precipitates intense feelings of rejection in the woman afflicted with BPD. Rather than listening to the explanation for the canceled activity, she perceives this as an attempt by the person to abandon her. She perceives rejection and these feelings manifest in angry, hurtful comments to the unsuspecting person who has a valid reason for canceling her participation in the activity. The BPD woman questions the truthfulness of the "excuse," and accuses the friend of lying and devaluing their friendship. These acts are self-defeating and commonly produce the opposite desired effect. The friend, offended by the accusations and tirade, chooses to terminate the relationship rather than deal with further episodes.

The person afflicted with BPD needs the presence of others to reinforce personal perceptions of self, regardless of the reality of the perceptions. They cannot be alone and utilize others to serve as a "mirror" of their self-perception, that is, as long as the other parties concur with the self-perception. Conflicting opinions precipitate the fear of rejection and abandonment and the ensuing inappropriate, frantic efforts to avoid the rejection.

A Pattern of Unstable and Intense Interpersonal Relationships Characterized by Alternating between Extremes of Idealization and Devaluation

Persons afflicted with BPD have a tendency to attach themselves to others very early in the acquaintanceship. They perceive the relationship as more intimate and enduring than the other person perceives the situation. The first date that ends with a sexual encounter is ripe for a delusional belief of enduring love. The woman, afflicted with BPD, develops a delusional belief that this first date encounter is a statement of enduring love from the man. She cannot understand when he leaves her bed to return to his own home. She demands an explanation and asks to see him the next day. The unsuspecting man calls her the next morning to tell her that he enjoyed their evening and asks her out on a second date for that evening. He may even send flowers. The die is cast. The woman's delusional belief of enduring love is reinforced.

The second date ends up in a similar sexual encounter. As he leaves her bed to return home, she will want him to stay for the night. If he does, the delusion is reinforced. If he does not stay, her fear of rejection and abandonment precipitates a verbal confrontation. Following his departure, she realizes that her behavior was inappropriate and develops a plan to reinstate the relationship. She bombards him with phone calls at his office the next day, and the man begins to realize the error associated with his two nights of intimacy with her. He decides the best course of action is to conclude the relationship with no further contact. He refuses to return her calls. She deploys frantic efforts to avoid the rejection.

To avoid any contact with this woman, he spends the night out with the "guys." When returning to his home he finds a message on his answering machine informing him that if he doesn't call her, he will be responsible for her death. Incapable of escaping the obvious "phony" threat, he calls her. In hysteria, she informs him that if he does not come over to her home immediately, she is going to kill herself. Frightened of the possibility that her threat may be true, he goes to her home and the ploy works and reinforces the delusion that it is truly an enduring love. This man is a victim to this woman's delusional attachment.

Unstable relationships are not limited to intimate relationships but also include family relations and friendships. The mother afflicted with BPD will place unreasonable visitation expectations on her adult children and grandchildren. Those who fail to meet her expectations are informed that they must not really love their mother or they would visit her more often and cherish their relationship together. The mother will also devalue and degrade those offending children to other relatives and friends.

Similar situations exist in friendships. The afflicted person expects that others are their "best" or perhaps "only" friend. They demand more time with this friend and are offended to hear that their "best" friend went to lunch or shopping with someone else. They demand to know why they were excluded. The final result is that their demands result in the end of the friendship and then the afflicted person devalues the relationship as insignificant to them and degrades the previous friend. This tactic protects their fragile ego and fear of rejection.

Identity Disturbance: Markedly and Persistently Unstable Self-Image or Sense of Self

The person afflicted with BPD will demonstrate sudden and unexpected changes in self-perception. These changes in perceptions of self may include radical changes in styles of dress, attitude, social preferences, hobbies, and preferences. If closely observed these changes are the result of perceived or real rejection and/or abandonment. It is an interesting dichotomy used as a mechanism to preserve a sense of self-worth or to reestablish a relationship with the person who has rejected them.

If a person afflicted with BPD is rejected or abandoned by another and the frantic efforts, including suicide attempts, are unsuccessful in reestablishing the relationship, the afflicted person may choose to change herself. She makes outward changes that she believes will bring back the lover, family member, or friend. In reality, the person who has abandoned or rejected her did so because of the behaviors associated with the borderline personality disorder.

Persons with borderline personality disorder are receptive to therapeutic intervention. Unfortunately, the therapeutic intervention is usually initiated following a suicide attempt. Acknowledging that it is one's personality and behavior that precipitates the rejection and abandonment is not easily accomplished. It is far easier to utilize anger and degradation of the other party than to accept the reality of one's own dysfunctional personality.

Impulsivity in at least Two Areas that are Potentially Self-Damaging (e.g., Spending, Sex, Substance Abuse, Reckless Driving, Binge Eating)

Due to the self-perception that they are not valued by others, persons afflicted with BPD, commonly engage in activities that are self-defeating and self-damaging. Suicide and self-mutilation are examples of self-damaging behaviors; however, they are not included in this criterion, but rather Criterion 5.

The behaviors associated with this criterion can best be described as defense mechanisms to the perceived affront of rejection/abandonment. Rather than facing the reality of the rejection and abandonment, they fill their lives with other activities. The behaviors are a neurotic reaction to the fear and anxiety associated with the perceived rejection. If a man rejects a woman afflicted with BPD, she overrides her anxiety by demonstrating to herself that there are a lot of men out in the world who desire to have sex with her and thus, she engages in promiscuous behavior.

She may indulge in substance abuse as a mechanism to escape the reality of the rejection as well as reduce her inhibitions that would normally preclude her from sexual promiscuity. She may indulge in a shopping spree, justifying her spending as she deserves it. She replaces the intimacy of another with new clothing that influences new feelings of self-worth. While these behaviors are short lived and bring no lasting comfort from the anxiety, some of them certainly have long-term implications.

Recurrent Suicidal Behavior, Gestures, Threats, or Self-Mutilating Behavior

These behaviors are the most dangerous. They have been excluded from the other criteria because these behaviors are not true attempts at taking one's life, but rather mechanisms utilized to keep others from abandoning her. Threatening self-injury if the other person abandons her is a powerful threat to ignore. The threat is usually successful at least once and, unfortunately, it reinforces the behavior and she will employ it again. Eventually, the other person recognizes the meaningless threat and ignores it. When the threat is no longer successful in achieving the desired result, an actual attempt is planned. The first attempts are weak excuses for a "real" suicide.

Persons who truly want to kill themselves are successful. Their attempt is neither half-hearted nor advertised. It is planned and successfully executed. They do not make a feeble attempt at suicide, nor do they call the person who abandoned them and inform him that they have taken sleeping pills. The person receiving the call considers it another cry of "wolf" and ignores it. Too frequently the half-hearted attempt is successful.

Affective Instability Due to Marked Reactivity of Mood (Intense Episodic Dysphoria, Irritability, or Anxiety Usually Lasting a Few Hours and Rarely More Than a Few Days)

Persons afflicted with borderline personality disorder commonly display instability in mood. For what appears to be no particular reason, they will be irritable, exhibit behaviors commonly attributed to depression, and anxious. It is not uncommon for these bouts of mood instability to last for hours or days and are not relieved by pleasurable experiences. They cannot be coaxed out of their mood and may react with intense anger at those who are attempting to offer relief. The fear of rejection and abandonment precipitates feelings of loneliness even while in the presence of others. It is a self-imposed perspective and those nearby relatives, intimates, and acquaintances experience the wrath of the person they are attempting to console or "cheer up." This is another self-defeating behavior. The moodiness and the angry responses to others motivate friends, caregivers, and intimates to remove themselves from their presence, thus producing the loneliness that they fear.

Chronic Feelings of Emptiness

Persons affected with borderline personality disorder express feelings of emptiness. It is a chronic rather than transient state. They have difficulty finding "depth" of self. They express that they cannot find a sense of purpose and a lack of value. They demonstrate an air of shallowness. They cannot describe issues or topics in which they have passion. This delusional quality increases their anxiety regarding rejection and abandonment. If they cannot find purpose and value in themselves, how is that others will? These perceptions fuel the instability mood and the subsequent angry, hostile responses to others, and the others depart. It is a self-fulfilling prophesy that the person with BPD predicts, and it is her behavior that causes it to happen. Consequently, they do feel empty and there is nobody around to dispel the delusion. The others have all escaped the sharp tongue and irritable mood.

Inappropriate, Intense Anger, or Difficulty Controlling Anger (e.g., Frequent Displays of Temper, Constant Anger, Recurrent Physical Fights)

The chronic feelings of loneliness and emptiness coupled with the fear of rejection and abandonment precipitate a "just under the surface" seething anger that can boil over at any time over insignificant issues. As the moodiness and irritability increase, the probability of confrontation increases. Their behaviors have driven away all potential friends and acquaintances, and their family and intimates maintain as little contact as possible. The adult children have excuses why they can't visit more often and the husband stays at work longer and socializes with his male companions. It is no longer a delusion that people are rejecting her; they dread the thought of reestablishing any form of relationship.

This is an accurate view in the mirror. It is at a point in time when suicide attempts are most probable and also when there is no relief from the anger that overwhelms her. She strikes out at the slightest provocation—a person who cuts her off on the highway, the clerk who inadvertently serves a customer that was behind her in line, and the daughter-in-law who hasn't called in 2 weeks. Younger women afflicted with BPD also engage in physical altercations. The husband that comes home from a softball practice and a few beers will incur her wrath and perhaps have to duck the thrown kitchen implement. Children who talk back to the young mother afflicted with BPD will experience the sharp tongue and a severe spanking or slap on the face. The man who breaks off an intimate relationship with her can expect angry, violent words, and striking fists. Unfortunately, the new girlfriend of the man who rejected the woman with BPD may also be the victim of assault.

Transient, Stress-Related Paranoid Ideation or Severe Dissociative Symptoms

Persons afflicted with borderline personality disorder may exhibit symptoms of mental illness at times of extreme stress, usually at the time of the rejection or abandonment. The person may exhibit paranoid symptoms that others are plotting against her and this entire act of abandonment was an act of conspiracy. Persons experiencing abandonment also talk as if they are having an "out of body" experience. They see themselves floating above the situation and observing it as an outsider. They cannot accept the reality of the circumstance, because this could never happen to them. These symptoms are usually short lived. The delusional belief that the friend, relative, or intimate will return precipitates a decrease in these paranoid or depersonalization symptoms.

Etiology and Course

The American Psychiatric Association indicates that "Borderline Personality Disorder is about five times more common among first-degree biological relatives of those with the disorder than in the general population" (DSM-IV-TR, 2000, p. 709). This prevalence among first-degree biological relatives lends to a discussion of nature versus nurture. It is further significant to reiterate that the disorder is commonly (75%) found in females.

Is there a nature connection? Are female children of a woman diagnosed with borderline personality disorder genetically predisposed to the development of the disorder? Is there a correlation with female hormones that predisposes women to develop the disorder at a much higher rate than males? In contrast, does nurture play a role in the development of borderline personality disorder? Is the development of the disorder based upon the direct nurturing behavior of the first-degree biological relative or is it a set of behaviors that is emulated by the observing female child?

Research on the heritability of borderline personality disorder demonstrates mixed results. The results on heritability of the aggregate disorder are not conclusive; however, there is much research that demonstrates the heritability of the aggressiveness and impulsivity. Further, there is definitive research that identifies a significant inverse relationship between levels of serotonin and aggression and impulsivity. In other words, as levels of serotonin decrease the probability of aggression and impulsivity increases. Consequently, one may conclude that the level of serotonin production is inherited and the resulting level of serotonin is directly associated with the probability of aggressive and impulsive behavior.

In contrast, there is research evidence that indicates sustained child abuse precipitates a reduction in the level of serotonin. Research has also demonstrated that with the manipulation of serotonin levels, aggressive behavior can be reduced. The inquiry remains; is the aggressive trait heritable through the levels of serotonin, or is it the behavior of the first-degree biological parent that reduces the production of serotonin, which in turn increases aggression and impulsivity?

The majority of persons receiving therapeutic intervention had it initiated following suicide attempts or aggressive behavior resulting in a violation of the criminal code (e.g., assault, domestic violence, and child abuse). The symptoms of borderline personality disorder subside with age, pharmacological treatment, and counseling intervention. While chronic in nature without therapeutic intervention, most persons afflicted with the disorder can be successfully treated with the symptoms remitting.

CHAPTER 8

Histrionic Personality Disorder

HISTRIONIC PERSONALITY DISORDER SCENARIO

Finally, the long years of hard work and sacrifice had paid off. John sensed the accomplishment as he entered the cocktail reception in celebration of his promotion to vice president of one of the largest insurance companies in the world. The accomplishment was further enhanced by the fact that at age 35, he was youngest ever to achieve the rank of vice president. In fact, no one had even approached the level prior to their mid-forties. John's personal celebration was not for the level of accomplishment, but rather the release from his self-imposed slavery.

John's father had abandoned his mother and three siblings when he was 10 years old. John and his siblings had grown up in poverty. He worked at fast food franchises, tended bar, and pulled third shift to make enough money for tuition and to help out at home. John attended the local community college, received his Associate of Arts, and then enrolled at the state university in the community. John's work schedule and persistence to be successful took its toll. There were only 24 hours in any given day and after work, classes, and studying, what little time remaining was allotted to sleep. John had no time for recreation or a social life.

He had attempted establishing a social life in his first semester at the state university, but he found his grades slipping by midterms. John reexamined his priorities and put aside a personal social life. His goals and objectives were clear. He wanted to be successful, not for the fame, but rather for the fortune that would raise his mother and him from the poverty of his youth. John had no delusions of winning the lottery; he knew hard work would prevail. Following receipt of his BA in Business Administration, he received a graduate assistantship to complete his MBA in finance from the same university. The graduate assistantship occupied more time than he anticipated and the faculty frowned upon his bartending to supplement his stipend as a graduate assistant. The stipend was sufficient to cover tuition, books, and a meager existence; however, the faculty believed his bartending left a negative perception of their department. Fearing the loss of faculty references upon graduation, John quit his job as a bartender, but secretively took a position with a local grocery store as a night stocker. John explained the circumstance to the store manager, who assured him that no one would see him and that he would keep his employment secret.

Days at the university turned into nights at the grocery store. The remaining hours were prioritized for study and sleeping. John had no social contacts, but he was able to keep his mother and siblings above the poverty level. John's intrinsic psychological needs were met through his altruism to his family. He needed nothing further at this time, but he dreamed of the day when he would have an income sufficient to take care of his mother and begin his own family.

Following graduation, the faculty pulled all of the strings for their "poster child" graduate. At 25, John received numerous high-paying offers, but chose, much to the dismay and embarrassment of the faculty, an entry-level position with an insurance company with its corporate headquarters in the same community. The insurance company was one of the larger companies in the nation, but the salary of the position John accepted was far below his other offers. While puzzling to his graduating peers, the faculty, and his new colleagues, there was method to John's perceived madness.

John had no desire to enter the "yuppie" world of the young executives in the "big player" metropolitan arenas. He watched these young executives from his position of bartender and found their lifestyle distasteful. He didn't judge them, he just chose something different. He was joyful to live at home with his mother, attend church with the family, and spend time with his growing siblings and their families. John knew his time would come.

A self-described workaholic, John put in 60 or more hours a week, volunteered to chair the most difficult assignments, and ignored the pleasures of his colleagues. In fact, John did exactly the opposite of all of his contemporaries. At quitting time, the young executives would meet at various "yuppie" taverns. Soon relationships were established and engagements were announced. John, being politically correct, attended the weddings and wished them well.

John's curious behavior did not go unnoticed. While his contemporaries often whispered about John's lack of a social life, the upper echelon executives noticed his no nonsense work habits. John "walked quietly and carried big performance." Further, he never would be accused of "kissing up" the upper-level executives as was the common practice of his colleagues.

John, at age 35, was unmarried and living with his mother. He didn't date or socialize with colleagues, but his work and productivity was impressive, sufficiently impressive to be promoted to vice president of finance. While his colleagues were getting married, having children, buying houses, paying mortgages, and attending little league soccer matches, John was positioning himself as the heir apparent to the retiring vice president of finance. By the time John's contemporaries realized his objective, it was too late. John was appointed to his dream position.

Quadrupled salary, company car, stock options, and an office on the top floor definitely change one's outlook in life. John could pay his mother's mortgage, purchase his own home, and start a life of his own. John had no intention of reducing his workload, because he was accustomed to it. He did, however, decide to initiate a social life.

John did not possess a sense of entitlement. He acknowledged that hard work, discipline, and dedication to an objective win in the long run. He was neither arrogant nor pretentious; he had just accomplished the achievement that he had worked for. While other young executives would make derogatory remarks about John to excuse their failure to compete for the position, this behavior was very short lived as John was their senior officer and controlled their future with the corporation.

As John entered the cocktail reception, he was immediately swarmed by his contemporaries and the recently hired entry-level employees. John knew that the plethora of congratulatory comments were really just a statement of political correctness. In fact, he was very much aware of the coveting of his contemporaries, and the "butt kissing" behavior of the recent hires. John would tolerate the behavior as he knew that his continuing future with the corporation was contingent upon his ability to have increased levels of productivity from these specific employees. As the evening drew later, he noticed a group of men of various ages crowded around an especially attractive and recently hired young female executive. John, hoping to appear social to his staff, ordered a martini, popular among the employees, and walked over to the group.

As the group opened to recognize his presence and authority, the young woman gregariously reached for John's arm, pulled him into the group center and coquettishly announced, "This is my new vice president." The bold announcement drew the laughter of the other men, but John's brightly blushing face, caused them to rapidly dissipate from the group. The young woman looked up at John and, with a tint, of embarrassment said, "Oops, maybe I should not have said that. Please forgive me if I have embarrassed you sir. My name is Tracy and I really do wish to congratulate you on your promotion." Tracy had not let go of John's arm and he was at a loss for words. Finally, he achieved some composure and assured Tracy that all was well, that he was not embarrassed, and he was appreciative of her sincere offer of congratulations. Hook, Line, and Sinker!!

Two martinis later, John asked Tracy if she was hungry and would she like to join him for dinner. Tracy agreed and they enjoyed a delightful dinner. Dripping spontaneity, eyes sparkling, and cute, but not immature, her silly laughter captured John. They talked throughout dinner, Tracy informing John that she had recently completed her MBA in finance from his alma mater and had only been with the corporation for a month. She talked of her career aspirations and her dreams to travel to exotic locations. John was absolutely captivated by this beautiful, intelligent, and spontaneous young woman.

Tracy accepted John's offer to drive her home and it wasn't until they were pulling up in front of her apartment building that she exclaimed that her car was back at the office. John, totally embarrassed for forgetting about her car, was fearful that Tracy perceived this as an ill-conceived plan to have him spend the night. Tracy sensed his embarrassment and remarkably indicated that this was her plan all along. Then she laughed, throwing back her long hair. Tracy unhooked her seatbelt, stretched across the console, and kissed John on the cheek. "Thank you for a wonderful evening. I'll just take a cab in the morning." Before John could say a word, Tracy jumped out of the car and jogged to the building entrance and disappeared behind the door. John was stunned and smiling from ear to ear. While he did not have much of a social life, he was not a practicing monk, but never had he encountered a woman like Tracy.

John used his status as vice president to obtain her home address from HR and the next day as Tracy returned from work, she found two dozen red roses and a card from John asking her out to dinner on Friday night. John picked up Tracy at 8 PM on Friday night and their evening would end Sunday afternoon, when John forced himself out of her arms and went home.

John and Tracy were married 3 months later.

Before the honeymoon in Hawaii had ended, John noticed that whenever he would leave the pool area, Tracy would get up from her chair and parade around the pool side in her tiny bikini, much to the delight of the men in the area, and much to the disgust of the women. Many a married man received a stern look and angry comment from their wife for their dropped jaw gawking at the perfectly proportioned and beautiful young woman. John would also observe her flirtatious little smile and giggle to comments from the men. He also observed her defiantly throw her head in the air as she paraded by the women sitting around the pool. It was incredibly obvious; Tracy was parading around to be the center of attention, and she was successful. As the days would go by, the women would drag their husbands from the pool area when Tracy and John arrived.

Following the evening's dinner and entertainment, John and Tracy would dance. Tracy's dancing was particularly seductive and everyone would watch her on the dance floor. Back in the honeymoon suite, Tracy became moody and showed little interest or pleasure in their sexual activity. John would reflect back to their lovemaking prior to the marriage and describe her as a little tigress and insatiable. Such was not the case following the wedding.

John finally confronted Tracy about her "strutting" behavior in front of other men and Tracy exploded with accusations of irrational jealousy. John immediately backed off and apologized for his inappropriate comment. Reluctantly, Tracy gave in to his continuous stream of compliments regarding her beauty and he agreed that he was jealous of those men watching her. Rather than continuing to confront Tracy's inappropriate behavior, he agreed that it was the men's inappropriate gawking and his irrational jealousy.

Tracy became pregnant early in the marriage and was happy to be the center of attention regarding her pregnancy until she could no longer hide her growing abdomen. While women were complimenting, men were no longer watching her. Tracy would theatrically tell John that she looked hideous and if John failed to comfort her with compliments, she would break into hysterical tears and accuse him of not loving her any more.

The pain of the delivery was the final insult to Tracy. She refused to breast feed her baby daughter and immediately hired a nanny to take care of the baby while she went to the private, co-ed, expensive health club to recondition her body back to it's tiny, undamaged form. Tracy continued at the health club long after she regained her seductive figure. She also exploded at John when he suggested that perhaps he should join her club and workout. It was obvious; this was Tracy's club, and not John's.

Whenever it would work to her favor, Tracy would take her, not John's, baby daughter "down off the shelf, dust her off," and go shopping where she would again become the center of attention. This continued until

Tracy realized that she was not the center of attention, her daughter was. Tracy would spend less and less time with her daughter and John and more time away from home. When she was home, she was moody and complaining, but her mood would immediately lift when John would suggest that they go out to dinner or a cocktail party.

Tracy was at top form at cocktail parties, always gathering a group of admiring men about her. When she could not acquire the center of attention or some other woman occupied it, she would dramatically throw back her head of long hair and loudly demand that John take her home because she had the worst headache. Her dramatic flair would gain the attention of others who would express concern and she would suddenly be well enough to stay. Tracy's appearance was paramount and she would take hours in preparation for the party and would always have a stunning new dress to wear. They would always arrive fashionably late and Tracy would make her entrance to the compliments of her beauty and her dress. Commonly the dress was seductively cut and exhibited her best features. Attending a cocktail party where another woman was wearing the same dress would result in their instant departure.

John finally caught Tracy having an affair with another man and divorced her. John and his daughter were victims of Tracy's histrionic personality disorder.

The American Psychiatric Association indicates that "the essential feature of the Histrionic Personality Disorder is pervasive and excessive emotionality and attention-seeking behavior" (DSM-IV-TR, 2000, p. 711). This disorder is most prevalent in females and it commonly develops in late adolescence and early adulthood.

The American Psychiatric Association identifies the diagnostic criteria for the histrionic personality disorder as follows:

A pervasive pattern of excessive emotionality and attention-seeking behavior, beginning by early adulthood and present in a variety of contexts, as indicated by 5 (or more) of the following:

1. is uncomfortable in situations in which he or she is not the center of attention
2. interaction with others is often characterized by inappropriate sexually seductive or provocative behavior
3. displays rapidly shifting and shallow expression of emotions
4. consistently uses physical appearance to draw attention to self
5. has a style of speech that is excessively impressionistic and lacking in detail
6. shows self-dramatization, theatricality, and exaggerated expression of emotion

7. is suggestible, i.e., easily influenced by others or circumstances

8. considers relationships to be more intimate than they actually are. (p. 714)

Uncomfortable in Situations in Which He or She is not the Center of Attention

Persons afflicted with histrionic personality disorder exhibit patterns of behavior that demonstrate their need to be at the center of attention and when not in that position experience anxiety. They have a personal perception that they are entitled to be the center of attention and when they are not, they feel unappreciated. They are very social, commonly gregarious, and talkative. They expect to be noticed by others upon their entrance into a room. When unnoticed, consequently unappreciated in their personal perception, they perform behaviors to position themselves in the center of attention. They will approach acquaintances and openly, but with a humorous and friendly tone, inquire why they haven't greeted them. They will boldly break into the conversations of others, introduce themselves to unknown parties, and generally move the entire center of attention upon themselves. "They commandeer the role of the life of the party" (DSM-IV-TR, 2000, p. 711).

Their compulsive need to be the center of attention may necessitate creating a scene. It may be a simple kiss on the cheek of a friend's husband or accidentally spilling their cocktail, or it may be more dramatic, including a feeling of light-headedness or faking a fainting spell. They may ask for a light for their cigarette in a nonsmoking area, thus positioning others to inform them that they cannot smoke in this area. They may conjure up some story that is sufficiently exaggerated to draw attention to them. When all attempts at securing the center of attention fail, they remove themselves from the environment, often leaving with a flair, which in itself draws attention. The sudden departure supports their egocentric need to be the center of attention and also demonstrates to others that they feel unappreciated.

Interaction with Others is Often Characterized by Inappropriate Sexually Seductive or Provocative Behavior

Sexually seductive and provocative behavior draws attention to the person afflicted with histrionic personality disorder. It may be directed at a love interest or it may be in social and work groups. The histrionic woman will openly flirt with a love interest, commonly displaying flirtatious behaviors more appropriate to intimate settings. Kissing, hugging, and caressing a love interest in the presence of others commandeers the center of attention. This behavior also has the potential to produce conflict.

The love interest may also be the love interest of another and this overt display of intimacy in the presence of other suitors can result in a confrontation. This behavior is also not limited to their love interests, but also to the spouses or intimate acquaintance of others. A married histrionic woman who fondly hugs and kisses the husband of another woman has solidly grasped the center of attention. Not only has she successfully grabbed the center of attention, she has also precipitated angry confrontations with the wife of the other man, as well as her own husband. The husband who was hugged and kissed is an innocent victim who must endure the inquisition of his angry wife. The husband of the histrionic woman is embarrassed by her behavior and concerned that there may be more to her relationship with this man. She has successfully acquired the center of attention at the social gathering, the two affected households, and has become the center of conversation among all the people who observed her inappropriate behavior.

The workplace is ripe for the seductive, provocative behaviors of the person afflicted with histrionic personality disorder. Vying for the attention of the immediate supervisor, the histrionic person will exhibit seductive, provocative behaviors. In full view of her colleagues, she will enter the office of her supervisor and sit down, cross her legs, and display her thighs. She may touch his arm in the presence of others or stare admiringly into his eyes. If she becomes the topic of conversation among her colleagues, she has successfully commandeered the center of attention. If the supervisor is receptive to her seductive, provocative advances, she has also angered her colleagues who may be interested in the promotion to which they all have aspired. The histrionic woman is less interested in the promotion than she is in being the center of attention, her primary psychological goal.

Displays Rapidly Shifting and Shallow Expression of Emotions

In order to maintain the center of attention, the person afflicted with the histrionic personality disorder must remain alert to changing conditions. The arrival of a next guest, a change in the conversation, or a demonstration of interest in another person requires rapid change on the part of the histrionic person. Consequently, they exhibit a flight of rapidly changing thoughts and lack the ability to remain focused on a particular topic in depth or for an extended period of time. Their emotionality is shallow and fake, particularly when it is absolutely required of them to demonstrate emotions to others. The newly arrived guest who informs the social group that she is pregnant receives warm acknowledgment and appreciation from others, but not the histrionic woman who has just lost the center of attention. Her congratulation to the pregnant woman is shallow and lacks true meaning. Similarly, most persons demonstrate true sympathy to the person who has lost a loved one. The histrionic person exhibits shallow but required emotion.

Consistently Uses Physical Appearance to Draw Attention to Self

One of the diagnostic criteria readily observed in the histrionic personality disorder is the consistent use of physical appearance to draw attention to themselves. It is relevant to point out that there is a direct correlation between this criterion and the criterion of sexually seductive and provocative behaviors. The histrionic personality disordered person does not dress outrageously such as football fans, but rather dresses with sexuality and seduction in mind.

Women afflicted with the disorder expend an extraordinary amount of time and money to look "just right." The familiar adage of "women dress for women, not men" does not apply to the histrionic woman. She dresses seductively for the attention of men and commonly dresses in a style that exceeds the appropriateness of the occasion. The histrionic woman will wear a cocktail dress to church or a funeral. She intends on drawing the sexual attention of men. She also draws the ire of wives and girlfriends.

Persons afflicted with histrionic personality disorder are not delusional in their belief that they are the most beautiful, as one is more apt to find with the narcissistic personality disorder. They do, however, recognize that one does not have to be a raving beauty to be "sexy." They identify their strong feature and dress to enhance it. If a histrionic woman has full breasts, she will enhance their exposure by wearing dresses and blouses with plunging necklines. If she believes that her legs are her best physical attribute, she will wear extremely short skirts or dresses with slits up to her waistline. If her figure does not have any particular extraordinary feature, but is proportionate, she will wear clothing that is tight form fitting, clothing that exhibits the proportionality of hips, to waist, to breasts.

The histrionic woman dresses to attract the sexual attention of men and the jealousy of other women. Husbands and boyfriends caught eyeing the histrionic woman are subject to an elbow in the ribs, a stern look, and subsequent lecture from their wives or girlfriends. "Hell hath no fury like a scorned wife or girlfriend." It is an interesting situation when two histrionic women attend the same social function. Two histrionic women cannot occupy the same space. If the room is large enough to accommodate two or more social groups, conflict can be averted. Let us now contemplate two histrionic women attending the same social function wearing the same cocktail dress. "Hell hath no fury like two histrionic women wearing the same cocktail dress to the same cocktail party." Clothing designers and jewelers significantly increase their wealth by designing numerous "single" dresses for the Oscars and Emmys celebrations. The designer who sells two identical dresses to women attending the Oscars experiences premature bankruptcy, and perhaps a threat to his life.

Women with beautiful hair will spend an extraordinary amount of time to highlight this characteristic. The same is true for eyes, cheekbones, etc. A characteristic of the young histrionic woman is the utilization of plastic surgery. It is easily understood that as women age they would prefer not to have the wrinkles and age spots associated with aging. These are not examples of histrionic women. Young women who enhance, increase or decrease, parts of their body and face to improve their appearance are exhibiting characteristics of the histrionic personality disorder. By no means should plastic surgery be considered a definitive demonstration of the disorder, but women who choose to alter their bodies and faces to enhance their appearance alone are subject to consideration.

This discussion of histrionic personality disorder has revolved around women because of the prevalence of the disorder with the female gender; however, men are also afflicted with histrionic personality disorder. The disorder in men is evident in the following characteristic. Narcissistic men may believe that they are the most handsome, but they do not expend extraordinary amounts of time and money on their appearance. They may spend a great deal of money on their vehicle, but not necessarily on their appearance. Histrionic men do. Some histrionic men spend an inordinate amount of time in the weight room perfecting exact muscular proportions of their bodies. They also wear clothing (or lack of clothing) to display their most extraordinary physical characteristic. Men with large perfectly formed biceps will always wear sleeveless muscle shirts. Men with perfect "six pack'" abdomens wear no shirts or leave it completely unbuttoned. Men with tight muscular buttocks wear tight (a size smaller) jeans, and men with powerfully built thighs wear tight spandex shorts. They wear the clothing for the same reason as histrionic women; to exhibit their sexually seductive bodies. Heterosexual men dress for the attention of women and gay men dress for the attention of other gay men.

Failure to be recognized for their appearance is disturbing to male and female histrionic persons. They are not receptive to criticism and can become very emotionally distressed.

Has a Style of Speech that is Excessively Impressionistic and Lacking in Detail

Histrionic persons utilize speech patterns that draw attention to themselves. The style of speech is seductive in tone and flow. It also lacks significant content. In other words, it is more important how one sounds, than what one is saying. The mellow seductive tone and presentation of Marilyn Monroe singing: "Happy Birthday Mr. President" to President John F. Kennedy is an excellent example of a histrionic person's use of tone and flow to impress others and gain the center of attention. It was a display of sexual seduction.

Shows Self-Dramatization, Theatricality, and Exaggerated Expression of Emotion

The world is a stage for the person afflicted with histrionic personality disorder. The primary objective of the histrionic is to always be at the center of attention. Theatricality is a common mechanism to achieve this goal. They control their environment through the dramatization of emotions. If they are not in the center of attention, they feel unappreciated, and then with dramatic flair express their frustration, depression, and despair. The expressions of emotions are greatly exaggerated with the intent of drawing the attention to themselves. They laugh too loud and too long, they cry hysterically, and engage in unnecessary argumentation.

This exaggerated expression of emotions often backfires on the histrionic person. Their theatrical behaviors are ever present. Relatives and close friends tire of their constant demand for attention and admiration, and their subsequent emotionality following their failure to achieve their goal. It is difficult for histrionic men and women to maintain romantic relationships or close friendships. Acquaintances merely tire of the same old behaviors. As the histrionic person ages they add new theatrical responses to their repertoire; however, the basic characteristic of exaggeration of emotions remains and the new responses are readily detected. Friends move on and relatives ignore them. Spouses divorce them.

Is Suggestible, i.e., Easily Influenced by Others or Circumstances

Needing to be at the center of attention, the histrionic person is particularly susceptible to suggestions from others. In the presence of love interests or persons of social, political, and economic prestige, the histrionic person readily accepts suggestions that they may pose. They do so without regard to rational processing, but rather because it was suggested by some person of perceived importance. By aligning themselves with a perceived person of importance or their love interest, they believe they are back in the center of attention.

This characteristic also makes the histrionic person susceptible to scams by experienced "con men." Some of the more successful "con men" seek out histrionic women. Wealthy histrionic widows are at great risk from the smooth talking gentleman caller who continues to keep her at the center of attention. They are the prey of the predator. Recognizing the need for attention and admiration, the suitor treats her like a "princess," craftily complimenting her on her beauty, intelligence, and of course, her "taste" in men. The characteristics of the histrionic personality disorder are reinforced by the actions of the suitor and she becomes more susceptible to his advances. His motivations are financial and not romantic; however, he will lavish romance upon her. The final diagnostic criterion for the histrionic personality disorder supports this contention.

Considers Relationships to be More Intimate Than They Actually Are

The need to be at the center of attention precipitates the delusion that intimate relationships are more significant than they are in reality. This is not only evident in romantic relationships as previously discussed, but also social relationships. Mere acquaintances become "best friends," particularly when the other person or persons have an enviable social reputation. The center of attention is transferred from the person with the enviable social reputation to the histrionic person. Simply, it is "name dropping," but to the histrionic person the relationship is real, not imaginary. The belief that the person with the enviable social reputation considers the histrionic person their "best friend" is a delusion, but it is reinforcing to the histrionic person. When she informs others of her "best friend" status, and it is not disputed, she achieves the center of attention.

Implications

Persons afflicted with histrionic personality disorder are at risk of distress when they are unable to achieve and maintain the center of attention. When theatrical attempts to control the environment are unsuccessful, histrionic persons may attempt more radical alternatives. They may become involved in novel activities at the suggestion of others; they may become sexually promiscuous, and may attempt suicide. The suicide attempts are not valid attempts to kill themselves, but rather a desperate attempt to gain attention acknowledgment, and appreciation.

When all appears lost, histrionic persons turn to professional clinical intervention. It is significant that the clinician recognize the histrionic personality disorder. Failure to accurately diagnose the histrionic personality disorder results in the therapeutic intervention reinforcing the disorder. Demonstrations of empathy, appreciation, and understanding reinforce the disorder. Confronting their intrinsic psychological need to be in the center of attention commonly results in the termination of the therapeutic intervention.

CHAPTER 9

Narcissistic Personality Disorder

NARCISSISTIC PERSONALITY DISORDER SCENARIO 1

Blake could not believe that his wife had filed for divorce. Furthermore, she was citing infidelity as the rationale for the action and was asking for full custody of the children. He contemplated the papers in front of him and then dismissed them. She wouldn't go through with it. She knew that he was the best thing that ever happened to her. She would not get the children, one red cent, and would be left broke and homeless. He would see to that. Blake would play her silly game and clobber her with a countersuit. The audacity of that woman to challenge him; she would pay the penalty. Blake pondered perhaps this was the best thing after all. He was tired of her complaining about him never being home and spending money on anything he wanted without any consideration of her or the children. Further, she was getting older and certainly didn't have that hourglass figure any longer. Plus, sex with her was infrequent and boring. Blake acknowledged he deserved better. He would counter and leave her behind.

Blake was the only child of a southern family of "old money." His grandfather had started a lumber mill, stripping the hardwood forests of the black walnut trees. His father diversified the company into furniture manufacturing. Following his father's death, Blake assumed the role of CEO. Blake had diversified the corporation further and coffers were overflowing with profit. He refused to go public, because the money was his and he would not have a board of directors nosing around in his business. It was his money and his alone.

Blake was raised as an overly pampered child. He could do no wrong. His misbehaviour was excused as someone else's fault and his parents always intervened to prevent the occurrence of natural consequences. When Blake was caught in possession of marijuana, his father sued the school district for unlawful search and seizure. Blake was pulled from the local public school district under the guise of its being inadequate for his particular genius. Blake was enrolled in a prestigious southern prep school. Blake was constantly on the edge of flunking out, but the enormous allowance he received allowed him to buy papers written by others, and cheat on exams. As graduation approached, the possibility of Blake attending an Ivy Leaque university was slim. His SAT and ACT scores were very low. Blake's father manipulated admission to a distinguished Ivy Leaque university by a generous contribution to the university's capital campaign.

Blake's university experience was no different than his prep school experience. Blake would rather drive his Porsche than attend class. He would rather party at the fraternity house than study. Relying on previous experiences, Blake purchased papers and cheated on exams. As a legacy from a very wealthy family, professors turned a blind eye to his academic misconduct. This reinforced his sense of entitlement. Blake just considered himself smarter and generally superior to others. If he did not excel in a specific activity, he would denigrate others for their participation. If he did participate and was less than perfect, he would blame others or the equipment for his failure to win. He was constantly accusing others of cheating. Blake could not comprehend losing. It was impossible.

Blake had a very active sex life. He would date a woman until they had intercourse and then discard her with no remorse. His handsome good looks, his Porsche, and pockets full of spending money attracted dozens of beautiful women. During his senior year at the university, he was determined that the homecoming queen should be his girlfriend; however, his playboy reputation was well known and she was reluctant to date him. Blake was persistent; he was entitled to this woman. She was a scholarship student and came from a working-class family. He persisted and her sorority sisters coerced her into dating him. The first date was uneventful and Blake was a complete gentleman, not even attempting to kiss her. Within an hour after she returned from the date, four dozen red roses were delivered. He paid a florist to get up in the middle of the night and deliver this beautiful bouquet. The attached note informed her that this was the most wonderful date of his life and he hoped she would consider dating him again. They began to date regularly and Blake even practiced monogamy.

The young woman was pre-med and had been accepted to Harvard Medical School. She would not be available for marriage for at least 6 years. This displeased Blake and they argued frequently. He wanted her to marry him and he would take care of her for the rest of his life. He wanted her to stay home, barefoot and pregnant, serving in the capacity of the southern belle. She adamantly wanted to become a physician. As graduation approached, they attended a fraternity formal. It was a wonderfully romantic evening with just a little too much champagne. The next morning she awoke naked in his bed. While she didn't remember the night before, it was of little significance, because they had been sexually involved for a few months. What she didn't know was that Blake had put an amnesiac date rape drug in her champagne. They had intercourse, but Blake did not use a condom. She was pregnant with Blake's child. Blake had won the argument; she would not go to medical school and they would marry.

Blake assumed the role of CEO upon his father's death. He immediately fired his father's secretary of two decades and hired a 20-something bombshell. Blake was having sex with her on her first day on the job. Blake fired everyone who disagreed with him and particularly everyone who was his father's loyal follower. This was Blake's company and not his father's. He couldn't care about mid-career employees that he fired without cause. Blake fired old employees, eliminated profit sharing, and hired new employees that swore allegiance to him. Blake kept the general manager on board with the threat of firing him if the profit margin fell. Blake controlled everything to his advantage. He had worked for his father for 10 years and believed that he was not receiving his proper share of the profit. That would now change. This was Blake's company and it was his money, all of it. He rationalized his behaviour as being entitled to it. He believed he brought the company from the dark ages to international success. It was his intelligence that increased the market position. His father was out of touch with contemporary economics and management practices. Blake had made it happen.

Blake drove very expensive cars, played golf nearly every day, and took extravagant business trips, always alone. He never took his wife and children on vacation, but encouraged them to frequently go on trips without him. He was just too busy to join them. When not at the golf course or on extravagant business trips, he would stay uptown at his apartment close to his business. His wife had no idea of the location and she only had his office and cell phone numbers, which he usually turned off when staying at the apartment.

Blake built his wife a beautiful home an hour's commute from the city. They lived separate lives. She raised the children and supervised the household staff. Blake ran the business and would come home on the weekends to entertain guests and attend country club functions. Blake's weekday life was a mystery to his family until his secretary showed up on the family front porch. She informed Blake's wife that she had been Blake's mistress for years, but when she asked Blake to leave his wife and marry her, he fired her.

When Blake arrived home on Friday evening, he was met by a summons server with a police escort. He was presented with a notice of his wife's intent to divorce and a restraining order. The police officer watched and waited while Blake packed his clothing and personal items. He was escorted from the residence and neighborhood.

Blake is afflicted with narcissistic personality disorder.

NARCISSISTIC PERSONALITY DISORDER SCENARIO 2

Jill adjusted the collar on her suit coat, brushed her hair, and reapplied her lipstick. She waited for the director of human resources to call her into his office. Her EEO complaint was being reviewed. She chose not to bring her attorney to this first meeting; she could always bring him later. She was confident that she could handle this bureaucrat alone. She knew this day was eventually arriving. She was adamant; no "glass ceiling" would stop her climb up the corporate ladder.

Jill first experienced the "good ole' boy's club" back in college. Despite all of the various "title" acts by the federal government, women continued to experience discrimination. Jill's father was a detective for the County Sheriff and she lived a lifetime in his stories. She patiently waited for him to come home from work and share his daily events with her. Jill had always aspired to be a law enforcement officer. She was the only child of her family and her father spent endless hours teaching her the things he knew best. They exercised together, she learned to handle all types of handguns, and earned a black belt in karate. Her father taught her that she was the best, unequaled by men and women, and was entitled to only the best.

High school was an adventure for Jill. She excelled in all of the women's sports, earning twelve varsity letters. When the high school varsity club refused her membership because she was a girl, she threatened to sue the school district. Jill proudly wore her varsity jacket even though the other female athletes declined. Jill denigrated the other girls as being afraid to tell the world that women were equal, if not superior to men. Her overt attitude and conduct alienated her from all of the students—male and female. The girls were embarrassed to be seen around her and the boys refused to date this girl, calling her a "walking time bomb," never knowing when she would explode with some commentary about her rights and that she was smarter, stronger, and more successful than her male counterparts. She would even encourage boys to take a punch at her. She longed to "kick their ass."

College was a replay of high school, with the exception of her attempt to try out for the football team. This caused a great uproar across campus. The female coaches and athletes were encouraging her to continue in her efforts to participate on the football team, while the male coaches and athletes were trying to dissuade her from trying out. Jill received ridicule from non-athlete female students, all male students, and even faculty. One freshman male pushed the envelope a bit too much and shoved her on the shoulder. Jill had been longing for this moment. Utilizing her secretive karate skills she proceeded to pummel the man into the hospital and then she filed criminal assault charges against him. The female athletes, coaches, and faculty raised her to stardom, and the rest of the college was terrified of her. She was willing to take any form of discrimination as high as necessary. Her father was right; she was the smartest, toughest, and most independent person in the world.

The remaining years of college reinforced her perception of absolute dominance. Following graduation, she made application to become a state trooper, the most respected, prestigious law enforcement agency in her state. She walked through the physical agility and strength evaluation, refusing to use the women's standards. She applied on equal ground with male candidates and finished in the top 5 percent of the academy class. As the highest graduating female, she was given her choice of post. Surprising to everyone, rather than taking a post in a quiet jurisdiction, Jill requested a post in the inner city, where state troopers were assigned to assist the local law enforcement agency. In return for the selection of the most dangerous post in the state, she parlayed her assignment to undercover narcotics. It was unheard of for a new, fresh-from-academy officer, particularly a woman, to be assigned to the exclusively male narcotics unit. The male officers vehemently protested, but with her history of EEO complaints discovered during the background check, the department was fearful of further complaints.

The male officers were brutal; first ignoring her, and then patronizing her. When the practical jokes began, she took matters into her own hands and flipped a particularly obnoxious officer over his desk. As he struggled to get off the floor, she told him she was filing a sexual harassment complaint against him and the unit commander. It was the last time that a used condom was left on her desk. The ridicule stopped, but no personal or professional relationships were formed. She was not invited to Friday's traditional choir practice (drinking at the police designated tavern). She was not even invited to the retirement parties, but this didn't bother Jill. She did not join the force to become a member of the blue bond, she had different goals. Jill wanted to be the youngest state police commander in the United States. While she felt entitled to the position, she worked hard to demonstrate that when she was promoted, it was not because she was a woman, but rather a "top cop."

Jill worked on the tough cases and volunteered for every special assignment. Within the first year, Jill had nearly doubled the number of narcotics arrests than the closest officer. While sitting stakeout, Jill studied for the Sgt. Examination. Knowing she did not qualify by years of service, she filed a union complaint of discrimination. She took the exam and scored a perfect score, unmatched by any other candidate. In similar fashion, she was offered her choice of post. Jill selected homicide. Her reputation preceded her and no one even considered childish initiation. Jill's persistence paid off and she passed the Lt. Examination in the first year. Her clearance rate on homicides was the highest in the precinct.

Jill knew that she was the best. She was intolerant of the apathy of other officers and filed complaints against them. She felt no remorse for officers that were demoted. She secretively served as a "mole" for the Internal Affairs Bureau (IAB) and was pleased to see corrupt officers fired and incarcerated. In the absence of fact, Jill would inform IAB of her suspicions of specific officers, who would come under intense scrutiny and surveillance. She selectively picked those officers who were in her way for promotion up the ranks. As they were sidelined as the investigations were conducted, Jill continued to receive promotions. Every time she would receive a promotion, she would parade it in front of the other officers, demonstrating she was a "top cop."

Jill also played the political angle. Every promotion, every major arrest, and every award made it to the media. Jill gave female reporters first "scoop" on stories, and they returned the favor by promoting Jill's image in the media. Copies of every article and electronic versions of TV news reports were sent to every female state legislator. The stage was set for the final push. Jill slipped an unsubstantiated rumor of fiscal impropriety by the state commander to the press. The media had a field day, demanding records of the state commander's use of the department's airplanes and helicopters. The state commander, with over the requisite number of years of service, retired rather than defend himself, acknowledging privately that there was a skeleton or two hiding in his closet.

Before the governor could appoint a successor, Jill's letter of application, replete with references from every female legislator, arrived at his office. Jill lacked enough years of service and bureaucratic experi-ence to be considered for the position of state commander. In hopes of averting political fallout, he offered Jill a position as deputy commander at the same time he appointed a senior male officer to the position of commander. Unfortunately, he neglected to offer an interview for the commander position and did not convene an interview with his appointed successor.

Jill filed a complaint with EEO and the female state senators and representatives brought the matter to the floor of their respective houses. The governor withdrew his appointment of the senior male officer and appointed Jill to the position of commander of the State Police. Jill is afflicted with narcissistic personality disorder, normally considered a male dominate disorder.

The *Diagnostic and Statistical Manual of Mental Disorders*, Fourth Edition, Text Revision (2000), describes salient features of the narcissis-tic personality disorder as "a pervasive pattern of grandiosity, need for admiration, and lack of empathy that begins by early adulthood and is present in a variety of contexts" (p. 714). Grandiosity or the act of being grandiose is "characterized by affectation of grandeur or splendor or by absurd exaggeration" (*Webster*).

Musicians refer to the most magnificent of pianos as "grand." Auto aficionados refer to the grandest of touring autos as "Gran Turisimo." These analogies accurately reflect the salient feature of the narcissistic personality disorder. Persons afflicted with this disorder firmly believe that they are, in fact, grand. They are exceptional, possessing character-istics uncommonly found in others. They believe that they are blessed with superior intelligence, beauty, creativity, and problem solving skills, consequently, they expect to be held in esteem by others.

This characteristic invades all of the aspects of their personality. Af-flicted persons who have uncommonly beautiful physical qualities trans-fer this unique quality to other aspects of their total self. Commonly they also believe they possess extraordinarily high intelligence, creativity, and problem solving ability. The Hollywood stars, admired for their beauty, conclude that their opinions regarding national and world politics ex-ceed the opinions of others. Naturally, since they are more intelligent, their opinions carry greater weight in the solving of social problems. The star,who travels to a foreign country to assert their political opinion which is in opposition to the official opinion of the national government, is an example of grandiosity.

The American Psychiatric Association identifies nine criteria that are characteristic of the disorder and are utilized in the diagnosis of the narcissistic personality disorder.

Diagnostic Criteria for 301.81 Narcissistic Personality Disorder

A pervasive pattern of grandiosity (in fantasy or behavior), need for admiration, and lack of empathy, beginning by early adulthood and present in a variety of contexts, as indicated by five (or more) of the following:

(1) has a grandiose sense of self-importance (e.g., exaggerates achievements and talents, expects to be recognized as superior without commensurate achievements)

(2) is preoccupied with fantasies of unlimited success, power, brilliance, beauty, or ideal love

(3) believes that he or she is "special" and unique and can only be understood by, or should associate with other special or high-status people (or institutions)

(4) requires excessive admiration

(5) has a sense of entitlement, i.e., unreasonable expectations of especially favorable treatment or automatic compliance with his or her expectations

(6) is interpersonally exploitative, i.e., takes advantage of others to achieve his or her own ends

(7) lacks empathy: is unwilling to recognize or identify with the feelings and needs of others

(8) is often envious of others or believes that others are envious of him or her

(9) shows arrogant, haughty behaviors or attitudes. (DSM-IV-TR, 2000, p. 717)

The American Psychiatric Association estimates that less than 1 percent of the general population is afflicted with the disorder and that between 50 and 75 percent are male. It is significant to note that the American Psychiatric Association estimates are based upon self-referral for treatment and court ordered evaluations. Justice practitioners suggest a much higher prevalence of the disorder in the general population. Characteristics of narcissistic personality disorder are commonly observed in persons afflicted with antisocial personality disorder. Justice clinical practitioners commonly diagnose persons with antisocial personality disorder and do not include narcissistic personality disorder as co-existing.

A primary criterion for a diagnosis of antisocial personality disorder is the "failure to conform to social norms with respect to lawful behaviors as indicated by repeatedly performing acts that are grounds for arrest" (DSM-IV-TR, 2000, p. 706). Persons afflicted with antisocial personality disorder are obviously highly represented in criminal populations. The diagnosis of antisocial personality disorder overshadows the coexisting narcissistic personality disorder and, thus, is under reported.

It is significant to recognize that the American Psychiatric Association estimates that 50–75 percent of those persons diagnosed with narcissistic personality disorder are male. Further, the under reporting of the disorder in criminal populations suggests that the percentage of males is significantly higher than estimated. Clinicians, discussing the disorder in non-clinical terms, frequently refer to the narcissistic personality disorder as the "male ego disorder." The diagnosis is not commonly found in women.

Grandiose Sense of Self-Importance

Boasting and bragging about achievements is a common manifestation of this criterion. The narcissistic personality disordered person will often exaggerate the achievement and the talents and skills necessary to accomplish the achievement. The fish are actually smaller, the golf score does not include his self-permitted "mulligans," and his date was not as beautiful as he claimed. Accomplishments of a work group are his personal achievements and the group activity is not recognized. Published manuscripts become his personal intellectual property right and the role of colleagues is not acknowledged. Every idea is his "brain child" and he is the lead problem solver. He is the supervisor that claims his supervisory skills precipitated the increases in productivity, when in reality it was the employees' initiative that produced the achievement. He is the university professor who assigns the research activity to his graduate students and then "steals" the intellectual property rights as his sole property.

Preoccupied with Fantasies of Unlimited Success, Power, Brilliance, Beauty, or Ideal Love

The person afflicted with the disorder daydreams about his meteoric rise to fame and fortune. His or her preoccupation with unlimited success is not self-contained, but rather is discussed with all that will stand long enough for the speech. The quality often appears delusional, but not in the mind of the afflicted person. Even in the face of statistical data that demonstrates the improbability of his success, he stands firm in his resolve. Contemplate the minute percentage of basketball players that are drafted into the NBA with the highly disproportionate number that believe they will succeed. The undergraduate student who seriously claims his career objective is to become a Supreme Court justice is not acknowledging the minute number of attorneys that are appointed.

Adolescents and young adults often dream the "billionaire" dream, but most face reality as they mature. The person afflicted with narcissistic personality disorder does not. The college co-ed who models on the weekends and believes she will be the next supermodel will mature and recognize the reality of this unattainable goal. The 35-year-old woman who believes she will be the next supermodel is delusional. In the face of reality, they hold on to the belief, because their ego cannot allow them to fail.

Believes They Are "Special" and Can Only Be Understood by Other "Special" People

The delusional quality of being special serves a dual purpose for the narcissistic personality disordered person. Their self-recognition of their "special" or "unique" qualities predisposes them to looking for special recognition from others. They expect to be held in esteem and deserving of special service and consideration. Standing in line behind others at the deli counter is unacceptable and they will demand the special attention of the service personnel. Their behavior is commonly offensive to others; however, it is also commonly endured in order to reduce confrontation. Failing to require the narcissistic person to wait their turn reinforces their perception of being special and deserving of special consideration.

This perception of being special dictates that they should only be in the presence of others of distinction. Their physicians will be professionally recognized for their expertise. Their golf coach will be a retired PGA tour player. They will join the most prestigious country club that their finances will allow. They also expect to reside in the most affluent neighborhoods. When finances preclude this residential possibility or country club membership, they excuse their failure by denigrating the desired neighborhood or country club for their discriminatory and exclusive nature. Thus, residing in the neighborhood and belonging to the club within their financial means, they verbalize their contempt for the snobbish conduct of others and lift themselves to a position of recognition in their neighborhood and country club.

Their children will attend the best private schools within their financial means or if they cannot afford a private school education, they denigrate the private school and praise the qualities of the public school district in which they reside. Their children will see the orthodontist and wear unique braces—colorful and noticeable. The children will participate in athletic events in which they excel. The parent will also force their child's participation, demand their child have special consideration from coaches, and boast of their child's achievements in excess of the actual ability. If the child fails to perform to "first string capacity," it is the coach's failure to recognize the child's unique ability or lack of coaching skills.

Persons afflicted with narcissistic personality disorder expect to be in the presence of persons with social distinction. Ordinary persons are not capable of fully recognizing their special and unique qualities. Obviously most cannot be in the presence of persons of social distinction; however, the afflicted person will make others believe that they are. Attending a lecture, concert, or political rally affords them the opportunity to exaggerate their relationship with the distinguished person. The narcissist will manipulate the situation to afford a photo opportunity. This photograph is prominently displayed in their home or office where others will see it automatically. The photo alone demonstrates their special relationship and opens the door for them to exaggerate the reality of the relationship. The photo reinforces their delusional belief that they are special as well as demonstrating it to others.

Requires Excessive Admiration

Persons afflicted with narcissistic personality disorder require admiration in excessive quantities. This admiration serves as a mirror image of their self-perception of being special or unique. While they are certainly capable of maintaining this self-perspective without outside recognition, the admiration from others is a solid reinforcement. In the absence of admiration of others, they prompt the necessary attention.

They need others to recognize their importance, the quality of their performance, and how others admire them as individuals. Failing to receive the requisite admiration, the afflicted person denigrates others to increase their prominence, or they change groups. This need for admiration from others precipitates difficulties with other persons also afflicted with narcissistic personality disorder. Two narcissistic persons cannot occupy the same space. The collision is apparent and common in certain environments.

If one contemplates the number of narcissistic males that may belong to the same golf country club, the potential for confrontation is obvious. Both requiring excessive admiration, they cannot enjoy a round of golf, even in the same foursome. Obviously, there is the single best "tee shot" on every hole as well as the best approach shot to the green and the longest putt accomplished. Consequently, there really is only "one" best of these golf shots that can be admired and praised as the best. A narcissist cannot come in second. He must be the best.

When confronted with the obvious reality that his golf shot was less than "best," he will make endless excuses. He will overtly and loudly reprimand the caddy for giving inaccurate information regarding the distance to the green, complain to the green's keeper for the ill-kempt condition of the course, or verbally confront a member of the foursome for talking while he was making the shot. He may even demand the opportunity to redo the shot or give himself a free "mulligan." The situation is further exacerbated if wagering is associated with the round of golf. How then are situations resolved? There is only one club champion. Most golf country clubs, in recognition of these uncomfortable circumstances, offer a variety of alternatives. Club championships are divided into flights; groups that are established according to handicaps, thus allowing for a number of club champions. Best ball tournaments are favored by narcissists. They are cognitive that they are not the best golfer at the country club. Consequently, they pick, usually with some financial enticement, one of the club champions as their playing partner. While their personal ball may not win the hole or the tournament, their partnership with the club champion produces the "win" and the requisite admiration.

Should the narcissist lose, denigrating remarks or allegations of cheating by the winning team are commonplace. Finally, the safest mechanism for saving "face" is not playing in the tournament or club championship. They proudly announce that they will not be able to participate in the tournament because of a previous agreement to participate in an altruistic event such as the Special Olympics, or a luncheon engagement with a prominent citizen. They are praised and admired for their willingness to sacrifice their joy of gold for events of higher significance.

Has a Sense of Entitlement

The person afflicted with narcissistic personality disorder believes he is entitled to treatment above and beyond the ordinary person, even if the treatment is unreasonable. The narcissist expects to be seated at a restaurant without reservations or at a particular table of high exposure. He expects to be escorted to the table by the restaurant manager rather than the hostess who seats all of the other customers. He expects the bartender to remember his "usual" cocktail made to his precise specifications. Even if prepared to perfection, he may send it back as being inferior and expect another.

The server is treated as a second-class citizen and undeserving of cordiality. If his meal is not served in his determined timely fashion or he considers it unsatisfactory, he returns it, half eaten, and demands his meal be "comped" by the management. He will leave no tip and then admonish the valet parking attendant for laxity in service.

The narcissist male will also have expectations of his female dinner partner. He believes that he is entitled to a sexual encounter following the conclusion of the evening's activities. He believes that he is entitled to a sexual encounter because he paid for her meal and theater tickets; he expects a sexual encounter because she was privileged to have his company for the evening. His special and unique qualities entitle him to the sexual encounter.

Interpersonally Exploitative

A salient characteristic of the narcissistic personality disorder is the exploitation of others. It is particularly significant because the exploitation is of persons with whom they have interpersonal relationships. It is a common characteristic of the antisocial personality disordered person to take advantage of others through criminal activity. The narcissist exploits personal acquaintances to his own advantage. They engage in activities that meet their personal goals and needs.

This characteristic is commonly encountered in the workplace. A narcissistic supervisor will demand work product from his subordinates and credit himself for the completed work. He excuses their contribution as being merely the activity that he brilliantly required of them and that they could never have accomplished the work without his direction. Individual members of a group involved in a group task may take credit for the work of all of the others and, if given the opportunity, will denigrate and downplay the contributions of the other group members.

The narcissist will exploit others as they climb the corporate ladder. The role of others is merely another rung to be climbed, regardless if he has to "step" on the others to meet his goals. This "stepping" on others on the ladder to success may include deceit beyond that of profiting from the contribution of others. Competing for a promotion, a narcissist may start a rumor that has negative implications on his competitor—inquiries pertaining to honesty, infidelity, sexual harassment of other employees. He initiates the rumor from a place of safety where his involvement is protected from detection. He excuses his behavior through his perception of entitlement.

Upon receipt of the promotion, he "humbly" accepts the admiration and congratulations from others. He further exploits his competitor by suggesting that it must have been a very difficult choice because their credentials are very similar and wishes him well in future opportunities.

The workplace is ripe for sexual exploitation. The "casting couch" and late night working hours are opportunities for the narcissist to offer financial reward and promotion for sexual favors. Young, underpaid, and naïve employees fall prey to the narcissist with significant authoritative and seniority status. Making a claim of sexual harassment is often dismissed by human resources personnel, particularly when they also are professionally subordinate to the narcissist. The fear of losing one's job further enables the narcissist to exploit sexual favors. Successful exploitation reinforces the narcissist's perception of entitlement and the cycle repeats itself.

Lacks Empathy

Another salient characteristic of the narcissistic personality disorder is the lack of empathy for other persons. This characteristic is the definitive statement of the egocentricity of the narcissist. The narcissist feels no concern for the needs and feelings of others. His needs are paramount and the needs of others are insignificant. This demonstration of a lack of empathy for others reflects the high degree of egocentricity and entitlement. As no other is as intelligent, attractive, or powerful, their needs and concerns are certainly less important than his; consequently, insignificant and not worthy of his concern.

The feelings of his wife, who is the victim of his infidelity, are insignificant, because his needs are paramount. He feels no empathy for his wife. Likewise, the feelings of the many mistresses' are insignificant in comparison to his needs, feelings, and concerns.

He will drive the luxury vehicle of choice while his children are wearing "hand me down clothes," but he justifies his vehicle as meeting his needs and helps continue his image of success. He is unwilling to spend time with the family, but he joins the local country club and plays numerous times a week. The money spent at the country club precludes the possibility of a family vacation, but he lacks empathy for their feelings. His needs are paramount.

On the upward climb of the professional ladder, his deceitful comments regarding his competitors are insignificant. He has achieved his desired goal and the feelings of the "also ran" are insignificant. His needs are paramount.

Envious of Others

The person afflicted with narcissistic personality disorder is envious of the power, success, beauty, and possessions of others. The reality of the success, power, beauty, and possessions of others that exceed his own is intolerable for the narcissist. He covets things that others possess and he does not. His perception of being the "best "or having the "most" is inaccurate and his fragile ego is endangered.

The solution is easy. Denigrate those who have more success, power, beauty, and possessions. The narcissist defames others by accusation that their wealth, power, success, etc. is the product of inheritance or gained through questionable activities. The narcissist stands straight as the person who "made his money the old fashion way, he worked for it" and it is clean money, not acquired by illegal means. He stands straight and tall to receive the praise and admiration of others, thus, saving face and reinforcing his ego.

Demonstrates Arrogant, Haughty Behaviors, and Attitudes

The grandiose sense of self-importance of the narcissist is readily obvious in his behavioral mannerisms. He struts his perceived superiority over others, often loudly announcing his arrival. He snubs service personnel who are not worthy of his acknowledgment. He looks down at others, demonstrating his perception of superior power, beauty, and success.

Etiology

Similar to the other personality disorders, there is no specific origin that explains the existence of the narcissistic personality disorder. It is commonly concluded that its etiology may lie in a combination of inheritable traits, behavioral modeling, and parenting. It is difficult, if not impossible, to identify a specific set of variables that precipitate the development of the disorder.

Proponents of the theoretical perspective that the origin of narcissism offer research studies that demonstrate that the incidence of narcissism is higher in persons who have a first-degree biological relative diagnosed with the same disorder. The American Psychiatric Associations indicates that of the persons "diagnosed with Narcissistic Personality Disorder, 50%–75% are male." (DSM-IV-TR, 2000, p. 716)

Consequently, utilizing the heritable traits and gender research, those males whose first-degree biological relatives, most likely their fathers, have been diagnosed with narcissistic personality disorder, have a higher probability of developing the same disorder.

Interestingly, developmental psychologists suggest that youth, predominately males, may develop a narcissistic personality disorder based upon the modeling of the symptomatic behaviors of a person diagnosed with the disorder. Albert Bandura (1974) proposes that it is not necessary for an individual to directly experience a behavior in order to understand the rewards or consequences associated with the said behavior. Individuals learn behavior by observing others perform the behavior. They watch and learn the nuances of the behavior and they observe the rewards and consequences received by the person who performed the behavior. If the outcome for the behavior appears to have a pleasing reward that meets the needs of the individual who performed the behavior, they are more apt to attempt the behavior themselves. If they observe a negative consequence received by the person who performed the behavior, they are less apt to perform the behavior.

Further, if the individual observing the behavior perceives the negative consequence as the result of a poor execution of the behavior, he learns to modify his execution of the behavior in hope of obtaining the desired reward. Rational persons perform behaviors with intent, intent to meet their intrinsic psychological needs. These behaviors are performed because the perceived result is pleasurable. Rational persons do not authentically perform behaviors that are distinctly unpleasant or fail to meet their intrinsic needs.

A child or youth watches as his older sibling or father performs a behavior and observes the subsequent reward or consequence the sibling or father receives. The youth evaluates the situation and the behavioral trait becomes part of his catalogue of experiential data to draw upon. If the older sibling or father is diagnosed with narcissistic personality disorder, they will exhibit behaviors typical of the disorder. If the person exhibiting the behavior experiences a reward, the observing son or sibling has identified a behavior that meets desired needs without a negative consequence, and will begin to exhibit the behavior himself.

This lends to an interesting inquiry. Even though the modeled behavior is characteristic of the narcissistic personality disorder, is the person who has adopted these behaviors through modeling a disordered person? The American Psychiatric Association recognizes this potential and addresses the issue. "Only when the traits are inflexible, maladaptive, and persisting and cause significant functional impairment or subjective distress do they constitute Narcissistic Personality Disorder" (DSM-IV-TR, 2000, p. 717).

This statement provides insight into the capacity for therapeutic intervention with the persons exhibiting behaviors characteristic of the narcissistic personality disorder. The narcissistic personality disorder, similar to other personality disorders is chronic and lifelong. Many persons afflicted with the disorder are very successful in their professional lives, and consequently do not experience distress. Those who experience professional or interpersonal distress precipitated by their disorder may seek treatment on their own or upon the advice of significant others. Narcissistic males that are facing divorce proceedings due to infidelity may find the consequences of their behaviors so personally painful that they choose to change the behaviors rather than suffer the consequences. It is also significant to note that persons afflicted with narcissistic personality disorders are very capable manipulators and their willingness to participate in therapy may be malingering and a mechanism utilized to escape the probable consequences.

Persons who adopt narcissistic personality disorders through modeling as a mechanism to adapt and often control their environment are flexible and more receptive to change. If an individual observes another receive a negative consequence for a particular behavior, he will drop the behavior from his repertoire. In fact, modeling works in a reverse fashion. It is common for an individual to eliminate certain behaviors when they are no longer necessary to meet his intrinsic needs. The young man who adopts certain narcissistic behavioral traits for success in college may find these behaviors are not necessary and perhaps viewed negatively, in the workplace.

Most therapeutic modalities can be successful with those individuals who are truly interested in modifying their behavior. In circumstances in which persons are reluctant to modify their behaviors, a consistently applied system of rewards and punishments is more effective. The adolescent that must endure consistently applied consequences for inappropriate conduct will, in time, choose to modify the behavior rather than face the carefully proscribed consequence. That is, if the consequence is personally meaningful to the person who must endure it. Removal of phone and email privileges, grounding, and driving restrictions commonly are consequences that adolescents find personally painful. Adolescents, like malingering adults, will challenge their boundaries, and consistency in application of rewards and punishments is requisite for behavior change.

CHAPTER 10

Avoidant Personality Disorder

AVOIDANT PERSONALITY DISORDER SCENARIO

Mike's father was constantly calling him stupid and clumsy. Mike's father was a master mechanic and Mike couldn't tell the difference between a wrench and a socket. Mike has an IQ of 140 and is exceptional in math and science and dreams of going to college and studying physics. Mike's father joined the U.S. Marines, completed his GED, and studied to become a mechanic. After his tour of duty, he came home and proudly displayed his U.S. Marine tattoo. Strong and handsome, all of the young women of the hometown were desirous of his attention.

With the help of a loan from a Marine veteran bank officer, Mike's father opened an automobile repair shop. He could repair any engine and his business flourished. His leisure time was spent building "muscle" cars, drinking beer with his car buddies, and dating every young woman who looked his way. One of the young women, Angie, became pregnant, and in adherence to the local culture and her father's insistence, Mike's father married Angie. Mike was born 3 months after the wedding.

Mike's father was not overwhelmingly happy about this state of affairs, but moving his business or divorcing Angie would be an economic disaster. Consequently, Mike's father did his best to live his current life and keep his single life as a discreet night and weekend hobby. He continued to build racecars, drink beer, and sneak out of town for a little infidelity. When he was home, he was miserable and Angie and Mike would pay the penalty of being his burden to carry. He drank every night and would strike Angie if she complained. Angie was fearful of leaving Mike with his father in fear he would hurt the child. He was always complaining about Mike's crying and telling Angie to shut him up or he would give him something to cry about.

Mike grew up fearful of his father's wrath. Mike's father knew better than to strike Mike, because Angie would leave and the community, in disgust, would not patronize his business. It did not stop him from telling Mike that he was the most stupid, clumsy, worthless kid in town. Angie's support and encouragement of Mike was no match for the father's cruelty. Mike cowered at expressions of violence and soon the alpha male high school students found a new kid to bully.

Mike was not athletic and he had a tendency to gain weight. Angie would attempt to counter his father's cruelty with comfort food: ice cream, cake, and sodas. Mike's lack of exercise and athletic endeavor coupled with permission to eat anything he wanted, particularly when he felt anxious, precipitated the growth of an obese frame. Mike's obesity added fuel to the fire of his father's and the other student's ridicule, and in authorization from Angie, Mike would eat more comfort food.

While Mike found success in the math and science laboratories, he couldn't spend all of his time secluded in these classrooms. Mike would quickly go home after school and hide in his room; reading, working on math problems, and writing a fantasy "dungeons and dragons" type book. Mike finally graduated from high school and through the efforts of his math and science teachers, received a full ride, tuition, books, room and board, at a small but distinguished private liberal arts college. Mike anxiously waited the time to leave for school. His father's demonstration of wrath to Angie and Mike became increasingly more frequent the closer it came to his departure.

Mike enrolled as a freshman and moved into the co-ed dormitory. The female students lived in one wing, the males in the other and shared dining and recreational facilities. Mike's prayer to escape his father and the hometown bullies was answered, but his problems did not subside. Mike's roommate had arrived 2 weeks earlier for football practice. Mike had merely replaced one group of antagonists with another, and he had neither Angie to protect him, or a place to run from the ridicule. The ridicule turned into practical jokes in which Mike was the center of the humiliation. The students, male and female, joined in the laughter at Mike's expense. Mike dropped out of the prestigious school and returned home at the end of the first semester.

This was exactly what his father predicted that his son, Mike, the total failure, would do. The ridicule was relentless, but short lived. With the help of a high school teacher, Mike received a full ride scholarship to the local community college. Mike moved into a studio apartment, enrolled in classes, and took a job as a clerk at the shopping center. Everything appeared to be on the upslope for Mike. The ridicule was still there, but he could escape in his own apartment. He also talked his employer into allowing him to work in the stockroom conducting inventory audits. He was not very successful with the customers and was constantly criticized by the supervisors. He was successful when avoiding social contact in the workplace.

Mike found it easier to escape what he believed were the negative judgmental looks of others than involve himself in clubs and other student activities. Mike viewed himself as socially inept, and disliked by others, consequently, he avoided social contact with others. Mike liked living in his apartment by himself. As long as he stayed in the shadows, he could actually walk to work and enter the stockroom through the receiving entrance. He would shop for groceries at late hours when few people were in the store and avoid eye contact with others.

Mike's dream of complete solitude was realized when the community college offered the entire curriculum online through the Internet. The scholarship paid for a computer and the Internet connection. He could now escape the probability of embarrassment in the virtual community college. The Internet empowered him to enter chatrooms and talk with others without ever meeting them. He could double check his spelling and grammar and take time to think out his replies. He could even create a new image. Mike became a scholar, researching every topic and applying the critical thinking skills that he innately possessed. At the encouragement of one of his college online instructors, he agreed to serve as an online tutor for students who were having difficulty in physics.

Mike was assigned a female student who probably should not have enrolled in the physics class in the first place. She was completely lost and closing in on a failing grade. Mike spent endless hours tutoring her and she was very grateful for his assistance in her receiving a passing grade. Her parents were also grateful for his tutoring assistance. The parents invited Mike to join them and their daughter for dinner at a local restaurant.

Mike was very reluctant to accept their offer, but they were persistent, and he agreed to join them. He agreed to meet them at the restaurant. Mike purchased a new white shirt and tie, pressed his best slacks, and polished his shoes.

Mike arrived at the restaurant early and was guided to a table reserved in the family's name. Mike could watch the hostess stand from his seat and observed an attractive young woman arrive with a couple that was certainly her parents. As the family were being guided to the table Mike stood up to greet them. They were awestruck by Mike's obesity and could not disguise their surprise. The father quickly composed himself and warmly greeted Mike with a handshake, but it was their daughter's reluctance to sit next to Mike that reinforced the negative perception of himself that was pummeled into him by his father and classmates. Mike excused himself from the table and returned to his apartment, where he was safe. He would not venture out again unless under circumstances he controlled.

Mike is afflicted with avoidant personality disorder.

The American Psychiatric Association identifies "the essential feature of Avoidant Personality Disorder is a pervasive pattern of social inhibition, feelings of inadequacy, and hypersensitivity to negative evaluation that begins by early adulthood and is present in a variety of contexts" (DSM-IV-TR, 2000, p. 718).

The APA establishes the following specific criteria for a diagnosis of avoidant personality disorder:

A pervasive pattern of social inhibition, feelings of inadequacy, and hypersensitivity to negative evaluation, beginning by early adulthood and present in a variety of contexts, as indicated by four (or more) of the following:

1. avoids occupational activities that involve significant interpersonal contact, because of fears of criticism, disapproval, or rejection
2. is unwilling to get involved with people unless certain of being liked
3. shows restraint within intimate relationships because of being shamed or ridiculed
4. is preoccupied with being criticized or rejected in social situations
5. is inhibited in new interpersonal situations because of feelings of inadequacy
6. views self as socially inept, personally unappealing, or inferior to others
7. is unusually reluctant to take personal risks or to engage in any new activities because they may prove embarrassing. (p. 721)

Caveat

While the American Psychiatric Association indicates that the disorder begins in early adulthood, there is a significant predictor of the onset that, if recognized, can be very beneficial in preventing the occurrence or severity of the disorder. No young adult awakes one morning afflicted with avoidant personality disorder; rather the behavioral manifestations grow over time.

Shyness, fear, and isolation begin in childhood and there are numerous variables that may cause a child to be shy. Children who are overly protected by a parent have a tendency to be become fearful of all strangers.

The increased incidence of stranger child-abduction by sexual predators has created a social hysteria among parents. The social hysteria has also precipitated legislative changes that are overreactive and may in fact exacerbate the problem. Law enforcement officers are not going to excuse sophomoric sexual misconduct such as "streaking" or "mooning" as an act of immaturity and stupidity. Rather than adjusting the conduct to "drunk and disorderly," they will explicitly describe the conduct, which in fact, is a criminal sexual conduct of displaying one's genitals. Prosecuting attorneys, concerned with the potential of releasing a potential sexual predator, charge the young adults with the criminal sexual conduct charge. Judges and juries, concerned with the same issue, convict the individual as a sex offender and he is placed on a sexual registry for the rest of his life. The probability of this young adult re-offending is zero, but his "stupidity" will now have a negative connotation for the rest of his life. He will always be a suspect.

The failure to rationally contemplate the "reality" of the behavior overloads the sex offender registry and dilutes the surveillance and supervision ability of the criminal system. Worse, at the time of child abduction, the majority of the persons on a sex offender registry are unlikely suspects and precious time is lost in the identification of the probable suspect group.

Every time an Amber Alert is initiated, parents all over the United States become more paranoid and overly protect and supervise their children. I am not suggesting that we should not supervise our children or educate them to the concept of stranger danger, but when the parent's paranoia isolates the child, the child becomes fearful of all unknown persons. The parent's anxiety is transferred directly and indirectly to the child. The child becomes shy and fearful when the parent tells them not to talk to anyone who the parent does not know. The child also becomes shy and fearful when they are not allowed to participate in age group activities—soccer, T-Ball, gymnastics, etc. It is the parents' responsibility to watch who is watching their children and act responsibly. Videotaping the audience at an age group event and examining the persons against the sex offender registry is more responsible than refusing their child to participate in the activity. Carefully checking the credentials of the volunteer swim coach is more responsible that refusing the child to participate on the age group swim team. Consequently, many children are shy and fearful because they are made that way, not born that way.

Children who are moved about or acculturated into a new dominant culture are also unsure of themselves. They do not understand the normative behavior of the new group and the shyness is natural. Parents and elementary educators have a responsibility to assist in the child's adaptation to the new environment. Few children are naturally gregarious in a new setting and adult assistance reduces their fear of nonacceptance. The failure to recognize and assist these children who are experiencing difficulty "fitting in" may precipitate the development of the avoidant personality disorder.

Avoids Occupational Activities That Involve Significant Interpersonal Contact, Because of Fears of Criticism, Disapproval, or Rejection

The avoidant personality disorder produces interpersonal stress and interferes with occupational activities. A person afflicted with this disorder will never secure employment in situations where group participation and activity is required. This person wishes to be left alone in their cubicle and not have to engage in group work related activity. What appears on the surface as either shyness or arrogance is in reality, the fear of failing or being criticized in the eyes of others. This reluctance to participate with colleagues in work and social activities may be an occupational hazard that results in a lack of promotion or positive performance evaluations.

Is Unwilling to Get Involved with People Unless Certain of Being Liked

The person afflicted with avoidant personality disorder will demonstrate the same behaviors in social settings. They are reluctant to meet and make new acquaintances because of their fear of rejection. They are more apt to maintain familial relationships and relationships that have existed for a long duration. They find comfort with people that they have grown accustomed to and are confident will not be critical of them. They are skeptical of meeting new acquaintances even though they are being introduced by a close friend. They are also concerned that their "old" friend will like the "new" acquaintance better and perhaps abandon them.

Shows Restraint within Intimate Relationships Because of the Fear of Being Shamed or Ridiculed

The fear of being embarrassed or ridiculed prevents persons afflicted with avoidant personality disorders from developing intimate relationships. This is a significant self-defeating symptom. As relationships become less formal and more casual, teasing and playful comments are more prevalent. The afflicted person fails to recognize that this is the natural progression from casual to intimate, becomes embarrassed, perceives it as ridicule, and terminates the relationship.

This experience reinforces their feelings of inadequacy and, consequently, they are very reluctant to allow a casual relationship to become more intimate. The other party obviously is interested in moving the relationship beyond the casual state and is surprised at its sudden termination. Once again, the afflicted person's perception of themselves is reinforced and the pattern develops into greater isolation.

Is Preoccupied with Being Criticized or Rejected in Social Situations

The person afflicted with avoidant personality disorder is overwhelmingly concerned about the potential for criticism and consequently modifies their behavior to completely avoid any potential for the criticism. They don't have to worry about being criticized in a social setting if they don't participate in the social setting. It is much easier for them to reject luncheon gatherings of colleagues rather than fear the potential for criticism. The afflicted person observes the social frivolity of office colleagues, which inevitably includes "good fun" humor in teasing. The afflicted person is terrified of bearing the brunt of teasing because it is delusional, viewed as ridicule. By isolating themselves from others, they cannot be the subject of ridicule. Unfortunately, the isolation also alienates them from their colleagues, and the luncheon or after work invitations cease.

These behaviors are not limited to the workplace. Friends and understanding relatives are few. Friends ask their afflicted friend to join them in a social gathering in hopes of widening their breadth of friends and reducing their fear of criticism, but the afflicted person is too fearful to attend. Extended family reunions and funerals are always avoided even at the cost of an angry parent. Families always have a member that takes teasing closer to ridicule. This self-imposed isolation also precipitates alienation from family and friends and the delusion of unworthiness is reinforced.

Is Inhibited in New Interpersonal Situations Because of Feelings of Inadequacy

The person afflicted with avoidant personality disorder cannot avoid all situations. As much as they would prefer to be a hermit, survival and success requires interaction with others. Invitations to the employers' Christmas party cannot be avoided. Attending a sibling's wedding cannot be avoided. There will always be a new social situation that requires attendance.

The afflicted person becomes extremely inhibited, avoiding contact with others at all costs. When forced into a conversation, they become incredibly shy and answer only direct questions with the fewest possible words. This behavior is manifested because of their delusion of being inadequate, and the subsequent response from others reinforces this delusion. If casual conversation is impossible, the other party moves on to someone else, someone who is less inhibited. This departure reinforces the feelings of inadequacy, and the circle repeats itself.

Views Self as Socially Inept, Personally Unappealing, or Inferior to Others

The person afflicted with avoidant personality disorder is the exact opposite of the narcissistic and histrionic personality disorders. They have delusions of being inept in social settings and this precipitates inhibition, which demonstrates social ineptness. They do not find themselves appealing and therefore how can anyone else find them appealing. This delusion manifests itself in an unkempt physical appearance. Why take the time, energy, or go to the expense of looking appealing to others if they are not appealing in the first place?

It is a self-defeating behavior that not only reinforces their delusion of inferiority, social ineptness, and lack of appeal, but also makes isolation possible. By acting shy and dressing unkempt, isolation is assured and they cannot be the subject of criticism. However, the criticism does exist because of the self-imposed behavior, but it is behind closed doors and out of earshot. Others ignore the afflicted person, isolation occurs, and the feelings of inadequacy and inferiority are reinforced.

Is Unusually Reluctant to Take Personal Risks or to Engage in Any New Activities Because They May Prove Embarrassing

Persons afflicted with avoidant personality disorder are very happy with status quo. They want to stay in their comfort zone and are very reluctant to attempt new activities that fall outside of that zone for fear of embarrassment. All persons are reluctant to attempt new activities for fear of failure or embarrassment, but most eventually, but reluctantly, do participate. All people draw their own personal lines and cannot be persuaded over the line, e.g., skydiving, bungee jumping, violations of law, etc.; however, the afflicted person can rarely be persuaded to try something new, even seemingly innocuous activities, e.g., a new card game, going to a new tavern, learning a new dance. The fear of embarrassment "freezes" them in their comfort zone.

Etiology and Course

There are numerous variables that precipitate the development of the disorder. The overly protective parent was discussed earlier. A child who is the recipient of emotional abuse from a parent is also predisposed to the development of the disorder. If a child is constantly and systematically told they are worthless, they begin to believe they are worthless. A child who grows up in the shadow of a very successful sibling is at risk to develop the disorder. Living under the constant reminder of "Why can't you be more like your big brother?" or "How can you be such a nerd when your brother is such a fine athlete and loved by everyone?" produces feelings of inadequacy. Fearful they cannot live up to their siblings' success, they do not even attempt. They accept their plight in life and isolate themselves to reduce the possibility of embarrassment and ridicule.

Children may also become at risk similar to post traumatic stress disorder. A youngster who is forced to recite in front of the class may become so frightened that they "wet" themselves or begin to cry. Either of these circumstances is highly embarrassing. Even the most caring and talented teachers will not be able to control the ridicule the youth will receive from other classmates. This one moment in time places this child at risk. The child may become school-phobic, refuse to participate in activities with other children, and isolate himself from the world of embarrassment and ridicule.

Persons afflicted with avoidant personality disorder are receptive and successful in therapeutic interventions when they can force themselves over the hurdle of being embarrassed at the need for outside intervention. Varied therapeutic interventions including behavioral, cognitive-behavioral, and psychoanalysis are successful in treating persons afflicted with avoidant personality disorder.

CHAPTER 11

Dependent Personality Disorder

DEPENDENT PERSONALITY DISORDER SCENARIO

Leaving home and attending college was Amy's worst nightmare. During her senior year of high school, all of her friends were intense with excitement over the thought of being on their own, away from their parents. Amy's social group was the class leaders—academically, athletically, and in popularity. High school was her most treasured experience. As everyone else discussed the variety of different curricula and colleges that offered the best degree programs, Amy felt her stomach knot up in anxiety. She gleefully carried on the exciting discussion and even identified her chosen course of study and relevant colleges. Not wanting to be different, she never acknowledged her fear of being away from her home and without her high school peer group.

Amy was terrified of leaving her parental home. She had no idea how she could make it on her own at a distant college without the support of her family and friends. She relied on her parents and peers to make decisions for her. Not only did she allow others to make significant decisions for her, but also minor ones, such as style of dress, dating preferences, and leisure activities. Amy could never be characterized as independent or authentic. She was very content when others would make decisions for her, and if she was asked her opinion, she would defer to others. Making an independent decision was anxiety producing.

Amy found a solution to the growing anxiety regarding choice of college. She was fearful to tell the group that she would rather go to the local community college and live at her family home. She knew she would be ridiculed by her peers as they frequently laughed about other students who chose the community college route for their higher education. Regardless of financial inability to attend a college out of town or an interest in an applied curriculum, Amy's peer group referred to them as immature and afraid to break their mother's apron strings. Amy, reluctant to be different, voiced in with similar ridicule. Amy was successful in hiding her fears, but the idea of leaving to go to college was a daunting prospect.

Finally, her escape mechanism appeared. One of her close friends decided to attend the conservative Christian University 30 minutes away to study nursing. Amy quickly changed her career interest to nursing and applied to the same university. Upon acceptance into the university nursing program, Amy asked her friend if they could room together in the same dormitory. The friend quickly agreed. Neither would have the uncomfortable experience of being alone at the large university and they registered for the same sections of the same classes. Amy's fears were gone. She could even go home on weekends and her mother agreed to come to campus weekly to take home her laundry. College wasn't going to be that bad after all.

The dormitory suites were designed for four students; two study/sleeping rooms for two persons, separated by a full bathroom that the four would share. Amy and her friend planned on how they would decorate their study/sleeping room. They shopped for matching sheets, coverlets, and drapes. Amy did not have any opinion and was perfectly content to have her friend pick out all of the items and even if she did not agree with her friend's choice, she joyfully concurred on the selection. They even shopped for clothing together, and her friend, naively, did not even notice Amy's strange behavior of buying the exact outfits.

As the date for moving into the dormitory came closer, Amy's anxiety grew in intensity. Amy began to cling to her mother, constantly wanting to be at her side. Amy was even willing to do chores that she normally would never volunteer for. She was desperate for her mother's nurturance. She continually made her mother reiterate that she would come during the middle of the week to pick up her laundry and that it was okay with her that she came home from college every weekend. Amy's mother thrived on Amy's attention, because the marriage was not fulfilling. Amy's father's leisure time was spent in the garage working on her brother's car. The father had a very close relationship with Amy's brother. Amy and her mother were equally dependent upon each other and her mother and father had no relationship between them. Amy's mother was as anxious of losing Amy's presence as Amy was of being separated from her mother.

Despite the tears, Amy moved into the dormitory and the two room-mates carefully decorated their room as planned. The other suitemates also moved in to their room. Both came from a great distance and knew no one. The suite mates were surprised when they met Amy and her roommate/friend. Amy and her friend had similar haircuts and their matching room décor seemed to come straight out of a Bed, Bath, and Beyond commercial. Despite their attempt to be friendly and receptive, their surprise produced wide-eyed stares and smirks. When they retired to their sleeping/study room they laughed and pondered whether Amy and her roommate were lesbians. As the two girls met other girls on the hall, they gossiped about Amy and her friend.

It was not long before Amy's friend noticed that she was being ostra-cized by the other girls. Consequently, she made a concentrated effort to separate herself from Amy. This was easily accomplished as she was very attractive and male students were always flirting with her. She ac-cepted an invitation to attend a fraternity party with a handsome junior football player. She didn't tell Amy about her date and Amy went home for the weekend. Amy's friend made sure to show off her date and acted seductive enough to change any preconceived perceptions that she was a lesbian. In fact, her slightly sultry behavior was discussed in fraternity houses and locker rooms around campus and she was inundated with invitations to party.

To further separate herself from Amy, she rebuked Amy if she wore the same or similar outfit even a couple of days later. Amy regularly dated in high school and was seeing a hometown boy on the weekend. Her friend knew that she was not a lesbian, but in an all out effort to destroy any connotation and suspicion, she asked the resident hall director to change her room. Amy was devastated by the separation. Amy begged her friend to stay and cried uncontrollably when she moved out. No one was willing to move in with Amy because of the perception of her sexual preference. Amy was terrified of being alone. She was afraid she could not take care of herself without the support of a roommate and now that the university environment was hostile. She could not even seek out a new friend. Amy felt worthless and helpless.

Amy stuck it out for two weeks and then, crying hysterically, begged her parents to let her come home. Amy was safe again. Her parents offered her nurture and support and did not let her make decisions on her own.

Amy is afflicted with dependent personality disorder.

The American Psychiatric Association (APA) identifies that "the es-sential feature of the Dependent Personality Disorder is a pervasive and excessive need to be taken care of that leads to submissive and clinging fears of separation" (DSM-IV-TR, 2000, p. 721). The APA specifically delineates the diagnostic criteria for the dependent personality disorder as:

A pervasive and excessive need to be taken care of that leads to submissive and clinging behavior and fears of separation, beginning by early adulthood and present in a variety of contexts, as indicated by five (or more) of the following:

1. Has difficulty making everyday decisions without an excessive amount of advice and reassurance from others
2. needs others to assume responsibility for most major areas of his or her life
3. has difficulty expressing disagreement with others because of fear of loss of support or approval. Note: Do not include fears of retribution.
4. has difficulty initiating projects or doing things on his or her own (because of a lack of self-confidence in judgments or abilities rather than a lack of motivation or energy)
5. goes to excessive lengths to obtain nurturance and support from others, to the point of volunteering to do things that are unpleasant
6. feels uncomfortable or helpless when alone because of exaggerated fears of being unable to care for himself or herself
7. urgently seeks another relationship as a source of care and support when a close relationship ends
8. is unrealistically preoccupied with fears of being left to take care of himself or herself. (p. 725)

Caveat

It is important to note that the symptoms described above must be thoroughly evaluated in relationship to age-appropriateness, circumstances like a medical condition, and cultural expectations pursuant to age and gender. A middle-age adult who moves back into residence with his or her parents for comfort and support is normally considered as age-inappropriate; however, a person who moves back to the parental home because he or she is recuperating from an injury or disease would not be considered age-inappropriate.

There are cultures that reinforce submissiveness by a particular gender. A young woman who is taught that it is a man's duty to work outside the home and that she must tend to home and hearth; meeting her husband's demands without question may appear as afflicted with dependent personality disorder, while in reality she is demonstrating cultural normative behavior.

Children cling to their parents for nurture, and protection from anxiety producing situations, however, there comes a time when the youth must sever those ties and begin to demonstrate independence. Adolescents are notorious for "rebelling" against their parents' rules, opinions, and wishes, but this is a normal developmental milestone. Obviously, there are differing levels of severity in rebellious activity and when behavior falls outside the criminal code; this rebellious behavior is no longer age appropriate.

In contrast, the adolescent who clings to a parent for care, support, and all decision making is demonstrating age inappropriate behavior. The diagnosis of dependent personality disorder is contingent upon the person's demonstration of fear and inadequacy to survive on their own. This statement assists in differentiating the person afflicted with dependent personality disorder from persons who may be exhibiting similar behaviors but for reasons of deficiency in intelligence or health, and cultural expectations.

Has Difficulty Making Everyday Decisions without an Excessive Amount of Advice and Reassurance from Others

The person afflicted with dependent personality disorder has difficulty in making the simplest of daily functioning decisions; what clothing to wear for the climate, what to eat for lunch, and which route to drive to a commonly known location. This behavior is a blend of feeling inadequate and the need for reassurance. The indecisiveness may draw criticism, which is injurious to the dependent personality disordered person, or it may draw an extra measure of nurture. It is contingent upon the framing of the inquiry and the mood of the care provider.

Needs Others to Assume Responsibility for Most Major Areas of His or Her Life

The person afflicted with dependent personality disorder needs someone to take care of them and make decisions for them. The fear of inadequacy motivates them to be passive and not have authentic opinions. Their comfort zone is one in which they are overly nurtured for their age, routine is commonplace, and in the absence of routine, someone else makes the decisions for them. They are always inclined to allow someone to make the decisions about their lives. The dependent personality disordered male reluctantly leaves his parental home unless he has the opportunity to marry a woman with dominant characteristics. Similarly, the overly pampered young woman expects to marry a man who will assume the role of her father and take care of her.

Has Difficulty Expressing Disagreement with Others Because of Fear of Loss of Support or Approval

The person afflicted with dependent personality disorder chooses not to disagree with others. The person is fearful that their contrasting opinion may appear inadequate and "stupid" and they are very fearful of losing their base of support and approval. Consequently, they appear to concur, however, in fact, they choose to passively sit back and not offer a differing opinion. They will always concur with the masses, unless their care provider (e.g., parent, spouse), is of the opposing opinion. They choose to agree with the care provider rather than risk the loss of support and approval.

This criterion produces anxiety for the young married adult who must choose the side of their spouse or the parent who has provided care and support over the years of childhood and adolescence. It is a no win situation; failure to respond is confronted and the afflicted person is demanded to demonstrate loyalty to each side.

Has Difficulty Initiating Projects or Doing Things on His or Her Own (Because of a Lack of Self-Confidence in Judgment or Abilities Rather Than a Lack of Motivation or Energy)

The person afflicted with dependent personality disorder is very reluctant to initiate new projects. The fear of inadequacy paralyzes the afflicted person. They have little or no confidence in their ability to initiate, organize, and implement a project. Consequently, they do not volunteer to take on responsibility in school, work, and social contexts. However, they are willing participants, as long as they are not required to assume responsibility. They participate if they feel adequately supervised. Unfortunately, this reinforces their self-perception of inadequacy and incapability of taking care of themselves.

Goes to Excessive Lengths to Obtain Nurturance and Support from Others, to the Point of Volunteering to Do Things That Are Unpleasant

The person afflicted with dependent personality disorder may be incapable of extracting themselves from abusive relationships. The young woman who is overly nurtured and informed that she is not competent enough to take care of herself will be attracted to a man whose is dominant and obviously is capable of taking care of her. Unfortunately these men are often also abusive—emotionally, physically, and sexually.

The dependent need for someone to take care of them overrides their opinions of normative behavior. They will not disagree or argue with the abusive person, fearful that they will be abandoned and unable to take care of themselves. They become victims of sexually sadistic men.

Feels Uncomfortable or Helpless When Alone Because of Exaggerated Fears of Being Unable to Care for Himself or Herself

The sense of helplessness is pervasive and the afflicted person develops paranoia of being alone and being incapable of taking care of oneself. It is not uncommon to find widows and widowers fearful of being alone. In these circumstances, the sense of inadequacy may very well be the truth and not a symptom of dependent personality disorder. The widow who has never worked, paid the household bills, or driven a car is rightfully fearful of being able to take care of herself on her own. The widower who has never prepared a meal or done the laundry is also rightfully fearful of his inability to take care of himself. Is this the dependent personality disorder, or a learned behavior?

The widow who learns to drive a car, balance the checkbook, and gets a part-time job negates the past by putting her fears aside. Likewise, the widower learns to cook and clean his clothes. The dependent personality disorder cannot overcome the fear as it is pervasive. They do not believe they can survive without assistance. These widows and widowers move in with their children or desperately search for a new companion that will take care of the part of their life that is missing.

These characteristics are not just common to elderly persons. Adolescents and young adults who cannot leave the parental home for fear of failing at independence are excellent examples of dependent personality disorders. Obviously some of them are malingering in order to have their parents continue to support them; however, some are just fearful to try it on their own. Parents who continuously allow their adult children to stay at home are not helping in the situation; in fact, they are reinforcing the person's perception of incapacity to take of themselves, and the disorder is perpetuated.

Urgently Seeks Another Relationship as a Source of Care and Support When a Close Relationship Ends

The person afflicted with dependent personality disorder panics when a care giving relationship ends. The recent college graduate who refuses to evaluate employment offers that take him out of his parental home is demonstrating this criterion. If forced to leave, he or she will feel a sense of urgency to find a new relationship that will replace the care provided by the parent.

The young woman may find herself desperately searching for a man to take care of her, in the same manner provided by her father. She may even expect to live in close proximity to her parents' home for the additional support and assurance of acceptance. The young adult man will look for a young woman who fulfills his dependency needs formerly fulfilled by his mother. He transfers his dependency on his mother unto his new wife. If the young bride takes care of him and fulfills his dependency needs, the disorder is reinforced. If the young bride refuses to fill the role of his mother and divorces him, the afflicted man will seek out a new woman to meet his needs for support and assurance.

Is Unrealistically Occupied with Fears of Being Left to Take Care of Himself or Herself

The person afflicted with dependent personality disorder is obsessed with "how will I live" or "how will I take care of myself." This criterion is a self-defeating behavior. The afflicted person requires such an excessive amount of reassurance, they actually drive the caregiver away and the delusion becomes the reality.

Etiology and Intervention

Children who are first-degree biological relatives of an adult diagnosed with avoidant personality disorder are at a much higher risk of developing the disorder than children raised in families with no persons diagnosed with the disorder. It is easy to conclude that the origin of the disorder is in parenting. A father who demonstrates his inability to take care of himself models the behavior for his children. The mother who provides all of the assurances that her husband requires, reinforces her husband's feelings of inadequacies and demonstrates to her children that their father is inadequate. Children also learn by emulation that if they perform similar behaviors they will receive the same care, support, and assurance that their father receives.

Dependent personality disorder is more commonly found in clinical settings than the other disorders. Persons afflicted with the disorder are receptive to therapeutic intervention, but significant caution must be exercised. The afflicted person may very easily develop a dependency on the therapist and believe that they can't make it on their own without the assistance of their therapist.

CHAPTER 12

Obsessive-Compulsive Personality Disorder (OCPD)

OBSESSIVE-COMPULSIVE PERSONALITY DISORDER SCENARIO

John woke to the classical music channel on his alarm clock/radio at 5:45 AM. He rises at 5:45 AM every workday, Monday to Friday. John neatly folds the blankets and pulls the thread barren quilt over the bed. He follows his normal routine; making a pot of coffee, carefully measuring out the coffee grounds, sliding a table knife across the measuring spoon to exact the amount, and pours the exact volume of cold water from the refrigerator in the coffee maker.

As the coffee maker brews the coffee, John shaves and showers, and adorns his robe at exactly the moment the coffee maker beeps the end of the brewing cycle. Before he pours himself a cup, he peeks through the apartment door peephole, unlocks a number of deadbolts, opens the door, and retrieves the morning paper. He stares in contempt at the headline announcing today's expected protest favoring abortion rights.

After his normal two eggs, bacon, toast, and second cup of coffee, the parts of the news that meet with his opinions and standards has been read and then he dresses for work. Every square inch of John's closet is full with clothing and shoes. John routinely gains weight and then goes on crash diets. His closet is full of clothing of varying sizes and most are very old. The styles are a decade or more old, but John knows his weight will rise and fall again, and leisure suits will again become the rage.

John's apartment looks like a Skinner maze with stacks of books, magazines, and newspapers not only filling every nook and cranny, but also dividing the room into paths. The paths are also lined with worthless items that John cannot seem to part with. In anticipation of a "rainy day" circumstance, he saves everything that may conceivably have value to him later. He is also a miser with his money.

John is employed as an accounting clerk with a large bank in the financial district of his metropolitan community. John does not own a car because of the expense. He can afford to own a car, he just prefers to take the metro bus and save the money. He considers a car an unnecessary expense, one that would better be preserved for a time when he will really need the money.

John catches the same bus every day and expresses his displeasure to the driver if he is late to his bus stop. Very concerned about his timely arrival at work, John revised his morning schedule a year ago in order to catch an earlier bus and be assured of arriving before the 8 AM workday begins. There is no time clock to punch, but work rules are just that, work rules, and must be adhered to. He never leaves before the end of the scheduled workday, never exceeds his hour lunch and two 15-minute breaks.

John is always the first one to arrive at the office and he mutters his discontent with those employees that arrive late. He will never confront them and would never report them to his supervisor, but he does grunt his discontent as they arrive late, socialize with each other, grab a cup of coffee, and do not settle down to work until 8:30. Despite the stacks of old reports and accounting textbooks stacked in his cubicle, everything else appears in order. His pencils are the same length and carefully sharpened. John favors working alone and his productivity is very high, which results in positive performance evaluations and incremental raises. He does, however, not work well in groups.

Assigned to a work group under the direction of another colleague, the group miserably fails to accomplish their mission. John destroys the performance of the group activity by rigid adherence to rules, regulations, and repetitive revisions. In those situations in which John is assigned group leadership responsibility, he is hesitant, in fact, reluctant to delegate responsibility to other group members. John's overwhelming perfectionism drives his work group colleagues "crazy," but they all recognize that the assignment will be completed in a timely fashion and the work product will be excellent. Rather than argue with John, they let him do all of the work, staying over late at night and on weekends while the other work group members socialize and enjoy their leisure lives. John would rather sacrifice leisure time and work excessively. Consequently, John has few friends and little if any social life.

John maintains a rigid set of standards or rules, values, ethics, and morality that controls every aspect of his life. He is intolerant of the behaviors and opinions of others who do not demonstrate or verbalize values, etc., similar to his own. This inflexibility reduces the pool of potential friends and acquaintances. John either rejects them outright or his inflexible views alienate him from others. John has difficulty finding female companions to date because he cannot locate women with values similar to his. Whenever John has found women to date, he invariably scared them away because of his inflexibility and need to control the relationship.

John is afflicted with Obsessive-Compulsive Personality Disorder (OCPD).

The American Psychiatric Association indicates that "the essential feature of Obsessive-Compulsive Personality Disorder is a preoccupation with orderliness, perfectionism, and mental and interpersonal control, at the expense of flexibility, openness, and efficiency. This pattern begins by early adulthood and is present in a variety of contexts" (DSM-IV-TR, 2000, p. 725). The APA delineates the diagnostic criteria of the obsessive-compulsive personality disorder (OCPD) as follows:

A pervasive pattern of preoccupation with orderliness, perfectionism, and mental and interpersonal control, at the expense of flexibility, openness, and efficiency, beginning by early adulthood and present in a variety of contexts, as indicated by four (or more) of the following:

1. is preoccupied with details, rules, lists, orders, organization, or schedules to the extent that shows the major point of the activity is lost
2. shows the perfectionism that interferes with task completion (e.g., is unable to complete a project because his or her own overly strict standards are not met)
3. is excessively devoted to work and productivity to the exclusion of leisure activities and friendships (not accounted for by obvious economic necessity)
4. is overconscientious, scrupulous, and inflexible about matters of morality, ethics, or values (not accounted for by cultural or religious identification)
5. is unable to discard worn-out or worthless objects even when they have no sentimental value
6. is reluctant to delegate tasks or to work with others unless they submit to exactly his or her way of doing things

7. adopts a miserly spending style toward both self and others; money is viewed as something to be hoarded for future catastrophes

8. shows rigidity and stubbornness. (p. 729)

Caveat

Prior to initiating the discussion of the individual criteria, it is significant to inform the reader that there is a significant clinical difference between obsessive-compulsive personality disorder and the obsessive-compulsive disorder. They are two distinctly different disorders and commonplace language usage of obsessive-compulsive does not differentiate between the disorders.

The obsessive-compulsive disorder is described by the American Psychiatric Association as "recurrent obsessions or compulsions that are severe enough to be time consuming (i.e., they take more than 1 hour a day) or cause marked distress or significant impairment" (DSM-TR-IV, 2000, p. 456). Striking examples of this disorder may include obsessing over cleanliness and, consequently, compulsively washing one's hands 100 times a day; obsessing over the media's continual discussion of child sexual predators, and, consequently, refusing to allow your children to leave the house.

The characteristic behaviors of the OCPD are observed and characteristic of a number of other disorders as well as cultural practices, economic circumstances, and situational emotional impairment, and therefore caution is requisite to an accurate diagnosis. The APA provides an excellent example of a characteristic behavior that clearly differentiates the obsessive personality disorder from other diagnoses. "A diagnosis of Obsessive-Compulsive Personality Disorder should be considered especially when hoarding is extreme (e.g., accumulated stacks of worthless objects present a fire hazard and make it difficult for others to walk through the house)" (p. 728).

Is Preoccupied with Details, Rules, Lists, Order, Organization; or Schedules to the Extent That the Major Point of the Activity Is Lost

Persons afflicted with OCPD obsess over trivial details to the point that the objective of the activity is lost in the process. Utilizing rules, points of order, and meticulous job descriptions results to the disadvantage of the work group. They become so consumed with the process set forth by the OCPD person that the work objective is never accomplished. This criterion is also obvious in social situations. The objective of a family union is the joy and delight of getting long, nearly forgotten relatives together to share time, reminisce, and catch up on each other's lives. When an OCPD person assumes the responsibility of organizing the reunion, the disordered person creates extensive details, rules, planned events, and timeframes. The obsessive adherence to the rules and schedule frustrates and angers family members.

The organizing family member is so intent on controlling the situation and demanding that everyone have a "good time," they order people around and do not allow for flexibility in the day's activities. Others' opinions fall upon deaf ears and the anticipated joyful event is ruined.

Shows Perfectionism That Interferes with Task Completion (e.g., Is unable to Complete a Project because His or Her Own Overly Strict Standards are not met)

Many corporations utilize team-building exercises as attempts to increase productivity in the workplace. Some corporations institute new management philosophies to encourage their employee's personal vested interest in increasing the corporation's productivity and profit. Logic dictates that profit sharing is the most logical and successful mechanism of increasing employee productivity, decreasing loss, and subsequently increasing profit. However, reluctant to share profit with the employees, some corporations suggest that a "grass-roots" movement to create a vision statements, goals, and objectives will be more effective. Work groups are assigned with the goal of writing mission statements, etc. These commonly fail because each individual has his or her own personal perspective as their goal and refuses to collaborate.

These workgroups are absolutely doomed to fail if a person afflicted with OCPD is assigned to the group. These individuals are perfectionists and are excessively checking and double-checking all of the potential alternative interpretations of each sentence. If the group is given a set of instructions to follow, the OCPD personality follows the rules in exact detail with no room for flexibility and authenticity in thought. The only final product is the anger and frustration of the other team members and management.

Is Excessively Devoted to Work and Productivity to the Exclusion of Leisure Activities and Friendships (Not Accounted for by Obvious Economic Necessity)

This is an interesting criterion to consider. It must be carefully examined in light of the individual and his or her career orientation. It is inappropriate to indicate a diagnosis of OCPD to the fresh out of law school attorney working in a private firm. The culture of the law firm may have an expectation of 60–80 hours of work per week for associates. Further, those associates desirable of future partnership in the firm may work even more hours to increase the possibility of partnership. This overwork may appear as obsessive and compulsive and society may even label the attorney as a "workaholic." In reality, he or she probably would prefer to be spending time with family and friends or being engaged in leisure activity.

The diagnosis is also inaccurate for those persons who must work all available overtime or two jobs to meet the economic needs of their family. Likewise, it is an inaccurate diagnosis for the person who really loves their work and finds great pleasure in working over leisure activities. While many find "play" enjoyable, there are many who find "work" more intrinsically valuable. Therefore, the defining characteristics that meet the criterion is that the person works all of the time, does not like the work, and excludes himself from family, friends, and activities that they do enjoy.

An excellent example of this criterion is the excessive cleaning of the garage floor to the detriment to their opportunity to play, and disciplining their child for walking on it with muddy shoes. When these individuals do play, they do so with excessive attention to details and rules. The game of golf is not a pleasurable event for the other three persons in his foursome. He is constantly thinking about his form and is explicit about the PGA rules. "Mulligans" are not allowed and kicking your ball away from the base of a tree is tantamount to criminal conduct. There is no such thing as a friendly fun round of golf.

Is Overconscientious, Scrupulous, and Inflexible about Matters of Morality, Ethics, or Values (Not Accounted for by Cultural or Religious Identification)

This criterion is often difficult to understand. This criterion is not suggesting that a person who abides by all of the laws of the land is afflicted with OCPD. The criterion defines persons who accept and follows all rules of conduct without question. Whether the rules are formally established in the criminal code, Monopoly board game printed rules, or moral standards accepted or indoctrinated, the afflicted person follows them explicitly. There are numerous examples which help to understand the excessive nature of this behavior.

While teaching a youth to play chess, there is no flexibility for error. If the youth takes his finger off the piece and then realizes the error of his move, the OCPD persons will not allow the youth to withdraw his move. If the state prohibits gambling, this includes playing poker with matchsticks as a violation. If their work schedule dictates that they will be at the office from 8 AM to 5 PM with an hour lunch break, the afflicted person will be there before 8, take exactly a 1-hour lunch, and not leave before 5 PM, even if they spent 3 hours working at home the night before. Their strict adherence to rules affects others as well. The OCPD person will judge the behavior of others and often negatively influence his relationship with colleagues. These persons do not consider mitigating circumstances or allow for flexibility. They are rigid in adherence to the perceived expectations.

Is Unable to Discard Worn-Out or Worthless Objects Even When They Have No Sentimental Value

Stacks of old newspapers, balls of bits of string, and the last of each roll of aluminum foil are hoarded by the person afflicted with OCPD. They do not fail to discard the items because they are lazy; they believe that they may have use for them in the future. It is not uncommon for the person to have difficulty moving through their room because of the accumulation of worthless items.

The American Psychiatric Association considers this criterion definitive in the diagnosis of OCPD.

Is Reluctant to Delegate Tasks or to Work With Others Unless They Submit to Exactly His or Her Way of Doing Things

The person afflicted with OCPD cannot collaborate with others. They are capable of working with others in group activities, but only if all of the members of the group follow his or her rules and expectations explicitly. They demand that the work be completed exactly as they dictate. This is not limited to the world of work. The OCPD father who is teaching his son to fish will demand that he follows his instructions explicitly, even down to threading the worm on the hook. The afflicted person will demonstrate anger to the other person when the instructions are not followed explicitly. The youth who fails to follow the instruction of the OCPD basketball coach may have to run extra laps or shoot 100 free throws until he can demonstrate the coaches' instructed technique. Creative thinking is not encouraged; it is penalized.

Adopts a Miserly Spending Style Toward Both Self and Others; Money Is Viewed as Something to be Hoarded for Future Catastrophes

Money is viewed in the same fashion as accumulated worthless items; it is not spent, but hoarded. The person afflicted with OCPD has his or her own view of necessities of life. Clothing that may be old and outdated still has utility and should be worn rather than spending money on new clothing. Clothing is handed down from one child to another. Shoes are still functional until the soles fall off, and many can be glued back on. The defining characteristic of this criterion is that money for purchase is available, but the OCPD person hoards it in contemplation of the inevitable "rainy day," when it will be really needed to survive.

Shows Rigidity and Stubbornness

This criterion is observed in all the previous criteria and is a defining characteristic. Persons afflicted with OCPD are inflexible, reluctant to change. They have their opinions and strictly adhere to them. Their inability to see the world through the eyes of another precipitates alienation and distress. Work, play, and life "in general" must be played out to their expectations.

Etiology and Intervention

It is most common that persons afflicted with OCPD have been nurtured in an environment with a dominant person afflicted with the disorder. The American Psychiatric Association indicates that males are diagnosed at double the rate of females, which lends credibility of an increased predisposition to develop the disorder in a family dominated by a person afflicted with OCPD.

The disorder generally manifests in late adolescence and young adulthood, and is considered chronic and lifelong. The rigidity and stubbornness characteristic of the disorder reduces the possibility of successful therapeutic intervention.

Conclusion: Severity, Comorbidity, and Blend

In closing this book on personality disorders, it is significant to reiterate that all diseases and disorders have differing levels of severity. Each personality disorder has its own severity continuum, with minimal disturbance on one end of the continuum and very disturbed or serious at the opposite end. This is particularly significant to acknowledge as one examines antisocial personality disorder and conduct disorder.

At one end of the antisocial personality disorder continuum, we find persons who violate social norms with no regard, remorse, or empathy for their victims. Their behaviors may include infidelity, tax evasion, and skimming from the top of their employer's cash register till. On the opposite end of the continuum, we will find individuals who likewise violate social norms with no regard, remorse, or empathy for their victims. Individuals at this end of the continuum commit rape, murder, and genocide. Will a person afflicted with antisocial personality disorder start at the least serious end of the continuum and move to the far extreme? Some definitely will, but the greatest majority will not. They will continue to remain and progress along the continuum until they decide to change their behavior. They do not change their behavior because they have developed a conscience, rather, they have come to a point where the perceived consequences for the behavior outweigh the pleasure they derive from committing the behavior. Unfortunately, with the case of antisocial personality disorder and conduct disorder, that point is not reached until after they have been apprehended, convicted, and imprisoned for a major violation of the law.

As you read and hopefully reread this book, you will find intimates, relatives, friends, and acquaintances that are demonstrating the criteria for some of these disorders. Knowledge rules, and knowledge is gained by observation and evaluation. If you do find yourself questioning the conduct and attitude of another, carefully observe without committing yourself. If you are currently in a situation that makes it difficult to elude or avoid the person, try to ascertain the level of severity by watching and listening from a distance. Many of these persons afflicted with personality disorders are very receptive to therapeutic intervention, while on the other hand some of these persons, contingent upon the specific disorder, are extremely reluctant to involve themselves in a therapeutic relationship.

It is also important to recognize that there is no "perfect" example of any of the personality disorders. Some individuals will only demonstrate a few of the diagnostic criteria, while others may vividly demonstrate a host of characteristics. Do not be fast to judge or attempt to diagnose. Just observe behaviors, demeanors, and attitude. The person presenting these behaviors may be experiencing a situational emotional impairment that will dissipate with the resolution of the anxiety producing circumstances.

Many persons may demonstrate the criteria for more than one personality disorder—antisocial personality disorder and narcissistic personality disorder are good examples. Therefore, it is prudent to observe behaviors rather than attempt to diagnose. The personality disorders may coexist or may have blended together in a single individual.

Appendix: Theoretical Perspectives

The examination and understanding of Personality Disorders is an enormous undertaking and has preoccupied and consumed the careers of thousands of mental health clinicians. In recognition of the audience, this author has attempted to dispel the myths of personality disorders. It was not the intention of the author to produce a comprehensive manual that would meet the needs of clinical practitioners, but rather to provide insight into the disorders for an audience that includes nonclinical service providers, undergraduate students, and the general public.

The theoretical perspectives developed and promulgated vary according to the psychologist's education, research, and experience. While some psychologists believe that persons who are afflicted with personality disorders were physiologically predisposed to develop the disorder, others believe that the behavioral characteristics of the disorder are learned, and consequently can be "unlearned."

This appendix is provided to give the interested reader a starting point to conduct a wider and deeper literature review of the theoretical perspectives of different psychologists. These psychologists are recognized for their contributions to the discipline. Many are deceased, but their theoretical perspectives lead contemporary research efforts. Most of the original theoretical perspectives have been modified by subsequent researchers. The following list of psychologists is not intended to be exhaustive, but represents those perspectives that this author finds relevant to the study of personality disorders. They are listed in alphabetical order.

ALFRED ADLER (1870–1937)

Alfred Adler, educated as a medical doctor, was an early follower of Sigmund Freud, but disassociated himself following recognition that they differed in their theoretical perspectives on the nature of man. Adler believed that man is motivated by his striving for future goals rather than being motivated by past experiences. Adler believed that man is a "whole" person who develops his own unique style of life. It is his creative self that strives for experiences that enhance his life perspective. He is cognitive and evaluates experiences and opportunities in relation to the self.

Man may also strive for unachievable goals and the subsequent failure may produce an irrational belief of inferiority. This lack of success is based upon an inaccurate perception of his abilities and an egotistically skewed view of the experience or opportunity. Adler also promulgated the theory that man was inherently altruistic for the purpose of correcting society and his efforts to serve and correct society compensates for his ability to accomplish personal goals and objectives.

GORDON ALLPORT (1897–1967)

Allport's contribution to the discipline was the proposition that some persons have specific "traits" that are uncommon in the general population. The study of personality disorders is the recognition that some persons have "traits" that are not commonly found in the general population. Allport also indicated that a person's behavior is indicative of these "traits." He cannot act in fashions that are alien to the "trait." If a person has developed the trait of submissiveness, he will respond to the environment in a submissive manner.

Allport posited that persons are not biologically predisposed to develop the "traits," but rather develop the traits over time and their relationships and experiences with the environment. Allport utilized steps of personality development similar to the works of others. He also attempted to describe the "mature personality" as an extension of his positive traits that are recognized, utilized, and most significantly, are realistic and rational.

ALBERT BANDURA (1925–)

Albert Bandura is considered one of the leading developmental psychologists. He is recognized for development and promulgation of his Social Learning Theory. Drifting from the strict school of behaviorism,

Bandura posited that it is not necessary for an individual to experience a behavior directly in order to learn it. Bandura suggests that individuals learn behavioral responses to environmental stimuli by observing the rewards and consequences that others are subject to for performing the behavior. Simply, a child does not need to directly experience the pain associated by touching a hot electric bulb, but rather observes his sibling experience the pain.

Bandura's Social Learning Theory is utilized extensively in understanding the proliferation of social structures. Youth observe the rewards and the consequences of gang affiliation from the perimeter of the gang's activity. Youth observe the lucrative nature of dealing with drugs and the rewards of fast cars, fancy clothing, and a harem of female admirers. They also observe the consequences of affiliation as gang members are murdered in drive-by shootings by rival gangs, as well as the consequence of arrest, conviction, and incarceration. These negative consequences serve as a general deterrent to some youthful affiliation, but many others ignore the consequences in preference for the gang life style. Similarly, a teenager watches his father "quiet" his mother's nagging by slapping her in the face. The slap produces the desired result, and the teenager utilizes the same behavior to make his girlfriend submissive.

Bandura's theoretical perspectives are utilized by school, law enforcement, and youth servicing caseworkers to not only understand behavior, but also to develop effective programs to serve at-risk youth. His perspectives also provide insight in understanding the statistical relationship that children of a biological parent diagnosed with a personality disorder are more highly predisposed to develop the disorder. However, Bandura's theoretical perspective forces one to question whether the child is genetically predisposed or is merely emulating the behavior of the disordered parent.

ALBERT ELLIS (1913–)

Albert Ellis is recognized for his development of the theoretical perspective of Rational Emotive Therapy (RET) and Rational Emotive Behavioral Therapy (REBT). Ellis' development of the therapeutic modalities is based upon his perspective that man is rational and cognitive. Ellis rejects the perspective that man is controlled by his environment, but rather, possesses the rational capacity to control his response to the environment.

When man does not accurately view or recognize the environmental stimuli, he responds in an irrational manner, which commonly results in an undesirable result. Ellis also posits that when man clearly examines the environmental stimuli, he can evaluate alternative responses and react in a rational manner, meeting his desired goals.

Ellis' theories assist in understanding personality disorders. The chronic nature and rigidity of the personality disorders prohibit the individual from clearly examining the environmental stimulation, assessing viable alternatives, and reacting in a rational manner.

ERIK ERIKSON (1902–1994)

Erikson is recognized for his work in child psychology and specifically his recognition of stages of development that are associated with socialization. As a child develops through childhood and adolescence, his experience with the social environment is instrumental in the development of his identity. The roles that a child adopts and subsequently experiences, success or failure within the social environment, precipitates the self-identity. Erikson acknowledged the significance of parenting and the social setting of school in the development of the identity. He also suggests that at each stage of development, the potential for crisis exists. As the identity is established, the child or adolescent has self-imposed expectations of success or failure. When the individual's experience in the environment does not meet his expectations, his view of his identity is questioned and in crisis. In contrast, if he meets his self-imposed expectations, his perception of self or his identity is reinforced.

HANS EYSENCK (1916–1997)

Eysenck is best known for his work in the analysis of psychopathy, which includes his development of a checklist to be utilized by clinicians in the diagnosis of the Antisocial Personality Disorder. Eysenck's work was controversial, based upon his theoretical perspective that psychopathy is a genetic trait and consequently children of a biological parent diagnosed with Antisocial Personality Disorder are genetically predisposed to develop the disorder. He rejected theories pertaining to development and learning.

SIGMUND FREUD (1856–1939)

No discussion of personality is complete without an acknowledgment of the contributions of Sigmund Freud. Freud's contribution to the discipline was varied, but it is his theory of personality that is relevant to the discussion of personality disorders. Freud divided the personality into three distinct structures: the Id, which represents inherited traits and instincts; the Ego, the part of the personality that relates the individual to the environment; and the Superego, or conscience.

Freud posited that the personality develops through a series of psychosexual stages. Freud related dysfunction to disturbances and experiences related to specific developmental stages. He posited that through a thorough understanding of the experiences and disturbances during the developmental stages, psychotherapy could be utilized as an effective therapeutic intervention. Freud recognized that unpleasant and undesirable experiences were commonly "hidden" beneath the surface and were released in behavioral manifestations that appeared as irrelevant to the current environmental experience. Persons suppressing a past unpleasant experience may displace their anger as an outlet. Freud contended that by understanding the source of the dysfunction, an individual could attain emotional and mental health.

ERICH FROMM (1900–1980)

Fromm is recognized for his recognition of the role of society in the development of an individuals' personality. Fromm was critical of Freud's failure to acknowledge that an individual lives within a society and that the individual is forced to accommodate his relationship with society, not just his personal needs, wants, and desires. Consequently, man's desires come into conflict with society's demands. Fromm further recognized that there were a number of characters an individual could adopt to adapt to society: some successful, some not as successful. Some of these characters leaned more in the direction of meeting the needs, wants, and desires of the individual, while some required submission to the demands of society.

R.D. HARE

Hare is recognized as providing empirical demonstration that psychopathy is physiologically precipitated. Hare conducted EEGs on adult males diagnosed with Antisocial Personality Disorder and normal adolescents. Hare's results demonstrated that the EEG patterns of Antisocial Personality Disordered adults were similar to those of normal adolescents. This discovery resulted in his development of his Maturation Retardation Hypothesis.

Hare explained that the human brain grows to its cellular capacity during puberty, the same developmental timeframe as adolescence. In the discovery of similar brain activity of Antisocial Personality Disordered adults and adolescents, Hare posited that the brains of the Antisocial Personality Disordered adults were arrested in development during adolescence, or maturation retardation. This hypothesis explained why some Antisocial Personality Disordered adults ceased their characteristic behavior without intervention. The brain merely began to mature.

Many clinicians find Hare's work relevant because the behaviors of the Antisocial Personality Disordered adults and adolescents are very similar; lacking in remorse, pathological lying, irresponsibility, need for heightened stimulation, inability to defer gratification, and egocentricity.

KAREN HORNEY (1885–1952)

Horney's theoretical perspective pertaining to anxiety and neurosis was extremely significant in understanding the relationship of fear and anxiety to behavior. Horney discussed the relationship of a child to its environment. Disturbances in the child's environment threatened the child's perception of security and the child demonstrated his displeasure regarding the anxiety-producing experience in a variety of behavioral manifestations: temper tantrums, crying, isolation, and aggressive behavior, etc. Her theoretical perspective has significance to adults as well.

When an adult senses the discomfort associated with an anxiety-producing situation, the natural reaction is to reduce the discomfort. Persons develop different mechanisms for eliminating the anxiety, which Horney described as moving toward the anxiety-producing stimuli, moving away from the stimuli, or moving against the stimuli. Failure to move or respond results in a continuation of the anxiety, and maladaptive behaviors are adopted to adapt: for example, substance abuse, phobias, displaced aggression, and depression, etc.

CARL JUNG (1875–1961)

Jung was a close associate and follower of the theoretical perspectives of Sigmund Freud. Interested in developing his own theoretical model, Jung dissolved his relationship with Freud in 1913. Much of Jung's work mirrors that of Freud with just a modification in terminology. Jung's research was directed at the relationship of psychology and religion. His primary contribution and change in direction for Freud's work was his belief that a person strived for equilibrium and stability, and thus was receptive to psychotherapeutic intervention for emotional well-being.

ABRAHAM MASLOW (1908–1970)

Maslow is notably recognized for his development of the Hierarchy of Needs. Maslow's theoretical perspective acknowledges the irrational drives of man: hunger, thirst, shelter, and warmth and that man must fulfill these needs before he can move on and up the pyramid of needs. This organized delineation of man's needs, wants, and desires assists us in understanding the concepts of need versus desire, as well as the concept of coveting. When all expendable income is consumed on basic irrational needs, desires go unmet and growth beyond the first step of the ladder cannot be achieved. Dissatisfaction increases when comparing one's life circumstance to another's. While Maslow posited that man naturally strives to achieve acceptance and growth, other psychologists contend that it is this inability to climb the hierarchy of needs that precipitates strain.

IVAN PAVLOV (1849–1936)

Pavlov is the father of behaviorism. Following the Darwinian principals of man's irrationality and response to the environment, Pavlov demonstrated through his research with animals that all behavior is merely a reflex to environmental stimuli. Pavlov's research was limited to an analysis of the conditioned reflex as research of the brain rather than research pertaining to learning.

JEAN PIAGET (1896–1980)

Piaget is recognized as one of the most significant developmental psychologists in the discipline. Piaget conducted extensive research on the cognitive development of children. He developed the most widely accepted model of cognitive learning. Piaget's model carefully charts children through stages of cognitive development and identifies specific skills that are indicative of different levels of cognitive capacity. Piaget's model is utilized extensively in determining children's cognitive growth against his established milestones. Due to his research, children with disabilities or developmental lags are identified and provided with special education assistance to compensate and rehabilitate them.

Piaget's research is also an invaluable tool in ascertaining the competency of children, adolescents, and adults. He pioneered the theoretical perspective that age is not relevant to cognitive competency.

WILLIAM SHELDON (1898–1977)

Sheldon is recognized for his research that supports his theoretical perspective that personality and behavior is directly related to the physique.

He identified three specific types of physiques and their related personality types. Consequently, he also supported the theoretical perspective that man is biologically predisposed to develop certain personality types.

B.F. SKINNER (1904–1990)

Skinner is probably the most recognized and celebrated American psychologist. His theoretical perspectives are also controversial. Under the broad statement that all behavior is learned, Skinner effectively dismisses the role of cognition and disease in behavior. Following in the theoretical perspective of Pavlov, Skinner spent an entire career demonstrating how behavior can be modified through the application of a system of rewards.

Skinner demonstrates little acknowledgment or interest in the etiology of behavior, merely in the modification of it. Skinner contends, regardless of the source of the behavior, it can be modified through the application of a system of rewards. His lack of interest in discussing the role of etiology, environment, and cognition on behavior is a source of considerable debate.

Bibliography

Allport, G. (1937). *Personality: A Psychological Interpretation*. New York: Henry Holt.

American Psychiatric Association (2000). *Diagnostic and Statistical Manual of Mental Disorders* (4th ed., Text Rev.). Washington, DC: American Psychiatric Association.

Ansbacher, H. L. and Ansbacher, R. R. (Eds.). (1956). *The Individual Psychology of Alfred Adler*. New York: Basic Books.

Atkins, M. C., McKernan, M., and Talbot, E. (1996). DSM-4 Diagnosis of Conduct Disorder and Opposition Defiant Disorder: Implications and Guidelines for School Mental Health Teams. *The School Psychology Review*, 25(3), 274–283.

August, G. J., Realmuto, G. M., Crosby, R. D., and MacDonald, A. W. (1995). Community-Based Multiple-Gate Screening of Children at Risk for Conduct Disorder. *Journal of Abnormal Child Psychology*, 23(4), 521–524.

Bandura, A. (1977). *Social Learning Theory*. Englewood Cliffs, NJ: Prentice Hall.

Bartol, C. R. (2002). *Criminal Behavior: A Psychosocial Approach* (6th ed.). Upper Saddle River, NJ: Prentice Hall.

Beck, A., Freeman, A., and Davis, D. (2003). *Cognitive Therapy of Personality Disorders* (2nd ed.). New York: Guilford.

Belknap, J. (1996). *The Invisible Woman*. Belmont, CA: Wadsworth.

Benjamin, L. S. (1993). *Interpersonal Diagnosis and Treatment of Personality Disorders*. New York: Guilford.

———. (1996). *Interpersonal Diagnosis and Treatment of Personality Disorders* (2nd ed.). New York: Guilford.

Binder, A., Geis, G., and Dickson, B. (2001). *Juvenile Delinquency* (3rd ed.). Cincinnati, OH: Anderson.

Blanck, G. and Blanck, R. (1992). *Ego Psychology: Theory and Practice.* New York: Columbia University Press.

Blinder, M. (1985). *Lovers, Killers, Husbands and Wives.* New York: St. Martin's Press.

Brenner, C. (1982). *The Mind in Conflict.* New York: International Universities Press.

Burack, J. A., Hodapp, R. M., and Zigler, E. (1998). *Handbook of Mental Retardation and Development.* Cambridge, UK: Cambridge Press.

Burgess, A. W. (Ed.). (1985). *Rape and Sexual Assault.* New York: Garland.

Buzawa, E. S. and Buzawa, C. G. (2003). *Domestic Violence* (3rd ed.). Thousand Oaks, CA: Sage.

Cassidy, J. and Shaver, P. (1999). *Handbook of Attachment: Theory, Research, and Clinical Applications.* New York: Guilford.

Chandler, J. (1999). *Oppositional Defiant Disorder and Conduct Disorder in Children and Adolescents: Diagnosis and Treatment.* Retrieved from http://www.klis.com/chandler.

Cohen, A. (1955). *Delinquent Boys.* New York: Free Press.

Cohen, A. and Short, J. (1958). Research on Delinquent Subcultures. *Journal of Social Issues,* 14(20).

Cohen, P. and Cohen, J. (1996). *Life Values and Adolescent Mental Health.* Mahwah, NJ: Lawrence Erlbaum.

Colt, G. H. (1998). Were You Born That Way? *Life,* 21(4), 38–42.

Crespi, T. D. and Rigazio-DiGilio, S. A. (1996). Adolescent Homicide and Family Pathology: Implications for Research and Treatment with Adolescents. *Adolescences,* 31, 353–367.

Crowell, N. A. and Burgess, A. W. (Eds.). (1996). *Understanding Violence against Women.* Washington, DC: National Academy Press.

Damon, W. and Hart, D. (1988). *Self-understanding in Childhood and Adolescence.* New York: Cambridge University Press.

Day, H. D., Franklin, J. M., and Marshall, D. D. (1998). Predictors of Aggression in Hospitalized Adolescents. *Journal of Psychology,* 132(4), 427–434.

Deary, I. A., Peter, A., and Austin, E. (1998). Personality Traits and Personality Disorders. *The British Journal of Psychology,* 89(4), 647–661.

Dobbert, D. L. (1981, January). Profiling and Predicting the Violent Offender. Paper presented at the meeting of the *National Conference on Serious and Violent Offenders,* Detroit, MI.

Douglas, J. E., Burgess, A. W., Burgess, A. G., and Ressler, R. K. (1992). *Crime Classification Manual.* San Francisco, CA: Jossey-Bass.

Douglas, J. and Olshaker, M. (1997). *Journey into Darkness.* New York: Simon and Schuster.

Eaves, L., Eysenck, H., and Martin, N. (1989). *Genes, Culture, and Personality: An Empirical Approach.* London, UK: Academic Press.

English, K., Pullen, S., and Jones, L. (1996). *Managing Adult Sex Offenders: A Containment Approach. American Probation and Parole*, 13(1).

Erikson, E. (1968). *Youth and Crisis*. New York: W. W. Norton.

Eysenck, H. J. (1967). *The Biological Basis of Personality*. Springfield, IL: Charles Thomas.

———. (1977). *Crime and Personality*. London, UK: Routledge.

———. (1981). *A Model for Personality*. New York: Springer-Verlag.

Eysenck, H. J. and Eysenck, S. B. G. (1975). *Manual of Eysenck Personality Questionnaire*. San Diego, CA: Educational and Industrial Testing Service.

Eysenck, M. W. and Keane, M. T. (1995). *Cognitive Psychology* (3rd ed.). East Sussex, UK: Psychology Press.

Flora, R. (2001). *How to Work with Sex Offenders: A Handbook for Criminal Justice, Human Service, and Mental Health Professions*. Binghamton, NY: Hayworth.

French, M. (1992). *The War against Women*. New York: Simon and Schuster.

Freud, S. (1926). *Inhibitions, Symptoms and Anxiety, Standard Edition*. London, UK: Hogarth Press.

Glasser, A. J. and Zimmerman, I. L. (1967). *Clinical Intepretation of the Wechsler Intelligence Scale for Children*. New York: Grune and Stratton.

Glueck, S. and Glueck, E. (1950). *Unraveling Juvenile Delinquency*. Cambridge, MA: Harvard University Press.

Goldstein, A. and Weiner, I. (Eds.). (2003). *Handbook of Personality, Vol. II: Forensic Psychology*. Hoboken, NJ: Wiley.

Goody, E. (1977). *Deviant Behavior* (5th ed.). Upper Saddle River, NJ: Prentice Hall.

Gosselin, D. K. (2003). *Heavy Hands* (2nd ed.). Upper Saddle River, NJ: Prentice Hall.

Grinker, R., Werble, B., and Drye, R. (1968). *The Borderline Syndrome*. New York: Basic Books.

Groth, N., Burgess, A., and Holmstead, L. (1977). Rape, Power, Anger and Sexuality. *American Journal of Psychiatry*, 134, 1239–1243.

Gunderson, J. G. (1984). *Borderline Personality Disorder*. Washington, DC: American Psychiatric Press.

Hare, R. D. (1970). *Psychopathy: Theory and Research*. New York: Wiley.

———. (1980). A Research Scale for the Assessment of Psychopathy in Criminal Populations. *Personality and Individual Differences*, 1, 111–119.

———. (1991). *The Hare Psychopathy Check-list Manual*. North Tonawanda, NY: Multi-Health Systems.

Harris, J. (1998). *The Nurture Assumption*. New York: Free Press.

Harter, S. (1999). *The Construction of Self: A Developmental Perspective*. New York: Guilford.

Hasslet, V. B. and Hersen, M. (1999). *Handbook of Psychological Approaches with Violent Offenders: Contemporary Strategies and Issues*. New York: Kluwer.

Hazelwood, R. R. and Warren, J. (1989). The Serial Rapist. *FBI Law Enforcement Bulletin*, 49–63.

Hinman, L. M. (Ed.). (1996). *Contemporary Moral Issues*. Upper Saddle River, NJ: Prentice Hall.

Hodgson, J. F. and Kelley, D. S. (2001). *Sexual Violence: Policies, Practices, and Challenges in the United States and Canada*. Westport, CT: Praeger.

Holmes, R. M. and Holmes, S. T. (2002). *Profiling Violent Crimes* (3rd ed.). Thousand Oaks, CA: Sage.

Horney, K. (1950). *Neurosis and Human Growth*. New York: W. W. Norton.

Horowitz, M. (1988). *Introduction to Psychodynamics: A Synthesis*. New York: Basic Books.

———. (1998). *Cognitive Psychodynamics: From Conflict to Character*. New York: Wiley.

James, S. H. and Nordby, J. J. (Eds.). (2003). *Forensic Science*. Boca Raton, FL: CRC Press.

Judd, P. and McGlashen, T. (2003). *A Developmental Model of Borderline Personality Disorder: Understanding Variations in Course and Outcome*. Washington, DC: American Psychiatric Association.

Kaye, D. H. (1997). *Science in Evidence*. Cincinnati, OH: Anderson.

Keeney, B. T. and Heide, K. M. (1994). Gender Differences in Serial Murderers. *Journal of Interpersonal Violence*, 9(3), 383–398.

Kernberg, O. (1975). *Borderline Conditions and Pathological Narcissism*. New York: Jason Aronson.

———. (1984). *Severe Personality Disorders*. New Haven, CT: Yale University Press.

Kernberg, P., Weiner, A., and Bardenstein, K. (2000). *Personality Disorders in Children and Adolescents*. New York: Basic Books.

Kiesler, D. (1996). *Contemporary Interpersonal Theory and Research: Personality, Psychopathology, and Psychotherapy*. New York: Wiley.

Klein, E., Campbell, J., Soler, E., and Ghez, M. (1997). *Ending Domestic Violence*. Thousand Oaks, CA: Sage.

Knight, R. A. and Prentky, R. A. (1987). The Developmental Antecedents and Adult Adaptations of Rapist Subtypes. *Criminal Justice and Behavior*, 14, 403–426.

Lachar, D. and Gruber, C. (1995). *Personality Inventory for Youth Manual*. Los Angeles, CA: Western Psychological Services.

Lane, B. and Gregg, W. (1992). *The Encyclopedia of Serial Killers* (Rev. ed.). New York: Berkeley.

Lazarua, R. and Forlman, S. (1984). *Stress, Appraisal, and Coping*. New York: Springer.

Leary, T. (1957). *Interpersonal Diagnosis of Personality: A Functional Theory and Methodology for Personality Evaluations*. Oxford, UK: Ronald Press.

Loranger, A. (1999). *International Personality Disorder Examination (IPDE)*. Odessa, FL: Psychological Assessments Resources.

Lykken, D. (1995). *The Antisocial Personalities*. Hillsdale, NJ: Erlbaum.

Magid, K. and McKelvey, C. A. (1987). *High Risk*. Toronto, Canada: Bantam.

Masters, W. H. and Johnson, V. E. (1966). *Human Sexual Response*. Boston, MA: Little and Brown.

Medows, R. J. (2001). *Understanding Violence and Victimization* (2nd ed.). Upper Saddle River, NJ: Prentice Hall.

Memon, A., Vrij, A., and Bull, R. (1998). *Psychology and Law*. Berkshire, England: McGraw Hill.

Millon, T. (1969). *Modern Psychopathology*. Philadelphia, PA: WB Saunders.

———. (1990). *Toward a New Psychology*. New York: Wiley.

Millon, T. and Davis, R. (1995). *Personality Disorders: DSM-IV-TR and Beyond*. New York: Wiley.

Millon, T., Simonsen, E., Birket-Smith, M, and Davis, R. (Eds.). (2003). *Psychopathy: Antiocial, Criminal, and Violent Behavior*. New York: Guilford.

Nathanson, D. L. (1992). *Shame and Pride*. New York: W. W. Norton.

National Center for the Analysis of Violent Crime (1992). *Investigator's Guide to Allegations of "Ritual" Child Abuse* [Brochure]. Quantico, VA: Author.

National Center for the Victims of Crime (2001). *The National Women's Study*. Retrieved July 5, 2002, from http://www.ncvc.org.

New Jersey Penal Code (1994). Megan's Law–NJSA.2C:7–1 through 7–11, L.1994, c.128. Retrieved from www.law.cornell.edu.

Nordby, V. J. and Hall, C. S. (Eds.). (1974). *Practice and Theory of Individual Psychology*. San Francisco, CA: Freeman.

Oldham, J. and Morris, L. (1995). *The New Personality Self Portrait*. New York: Bantam.

Olsen, J. (1974). *The Man with the Candy*. New York: Simon and Schuster.

Paris, J. (1994). *Borderline Personality Disorder: A Multidimensional Approach*. Washington, DC: American Psychiatric Association.

———. (1996). *Social Factors in the Personality Disorders*. Cambridge, UK: Cambridge University Press.

———. (1999). *Nature and Nurture in Psychiatry: A Pre-Dispositional Stress Model of Mental Disorders*. Washington, DC: American Psychiatric Press.

———. (2000). *Myths of Childhood*. Philadelphia, PA: Brunner, Mazel.

———. (2003). *Personality Over Time*. Washington, DC: American Psychiatric Publishing.

Peled, E., Jaffe, P. G., and Edleson, J. L. (Eds.). (1995). *Ending the Cycle of Violence*. Thousand Oaks, CA: Sage.

Pervin, L. (Ed.). (1990). *Handbook of Personality*. New York: Guilford.

Piaget, J. (1967). *Six Psychological Studies*. New York: Random House.

Reich, W. (1933). *Character Analysis*. New York: Simon and Schuster.

Reynolds, W. (1998). *Adolescent Psychopathy Scale*. Odessa, FL: Psychological Assessment Resources.

Robins, L. (1966). *Deviant Children Grown Up: A Sociological and Psychiatric Study of Psychopathic Personality*. Baltimore, MD: Williams and Wilkins.

Rolling, D. and London, S. (1996). *The Making of a Serial Killer*. Portland, OR: Feral House.

Rowe, D. C. (2002). *Biology and Crime*. Los Angeles, CA: Roxbury.

Rutter, M. and Smith, D. (1995). *Psychosocial Problems in Young People*. Cambridge, UK: Cambridge University Press.

Sadler, A. E. (1996). *Family Violence*. San Diego, CA: Greenhaven Press.

Schwartz, M. D. (Ed.). (1997). *Researching Sexual Violence against Women*. Thousand Oaks, CA: Sage.

Sgarzi, J. M. and McDevitt, J. (2003). *Victimology*. Upper Saddle River, NJ: Prentice Hall.

Shaw, C. R. and McKay, H. D. (1972). *Juvenile Delinquency and Urban Areas*. Chicago, IL: University of Chicago Press.

Sheldon, W. (1949). *Varieties of Delinquent Youth*. New York: Harper Brothers.

Siegler, R. (1991). *Children's Thinking* (2nd ed.). Englewood Cliffs, NJ: Prentice Hall.

Sroufe, L. (1996). *Emotional Development: The Organization of Emotional Life in the Early Years*. New York: Cambridge Press.

Stark, A. and Flitcraft, A. (1996). *Women at Risk*. Thousand Oaks, CA: Sage.

Steinberg, L. (1999). *Adolescence* (5th ed.). Boston, MA: McGraw Hill.

Sullivan, H. (1953). *The Interpersonal Theory of Psychiatry*. New York: W. W. Norton.

Tyrer, P. (1988). *Personality Disorders: Diagnosis, Management, and Course*. London, UK: Wright.

VanderZanden, J. W. (1997). *Human Development* (6th ed.). New York: McGraw Hill.

Van Wormer, K. S. and Bartollas, C. (2000). *Women and the Criminal Justice System*. Needham Heights, MA: Allyn and Bacon.

Wachtel, P. (1977). *Psychoanalysis and Behavior Therapy*. New York: Basic Books.

———. (1997). *Psychoanalysis, Behavioral Therapy, and the Relational World*. Washington, DC: American Psychological Association.

Warren, J., Reboussin, R., Hazelwood, R. R., and Wright, J. A. (1991). Prediction of Rapist Type and Violence from Verbal, Physical, and Sexual Scales. *Journal of Interpersonal Violence*, 6(1), 55–67.

Websdale, N. (1998). *Rural Woman Battering and the Justice System*. Thousand Oaks, CA: Sage.

Webster's Unabridged Dictionary (2001). 2nd ed. New York: Random House.

Wedding, D. and Boyd, M. A. (1999). *Movies and Mental Illness*. Boston, MA: McGraw Hill.

Weisheit, R. A. and Culbertson, R. G. (2000). *Juvenile Delinquency* (4th ed., Rev.). Prospect Heights, IL: Waveland Press.

World Health Organization. (1968). *International Classification of Diseases, 8th revision*. Geneva, Switzerland: World Health Organization.

Wrightsman, L. S. (2001). *Forensic Psychology*. Belmont, CA: Wadsworth.

Index

About the Author

DUANE L. DOBBERT is Professor and Coordinator of Criminal Forensic Studies at Florida Gulf Coast University. He is Series Editor for the Praeger series in Forensic Psychology. Dobbert authored *Halting the Sexual Predators Among Us* (Praeger, 2004).